Barnyard Buddies

in plastic canvas

By MizFitz

With Barnyard Buddies, you can bring your favorite farm friends indoors! If you love cows, chickens, or pigs, this is the book for you. Learn tips for stitching on plastic canvas, and create adorable, functional pieces perfect for gifting or keeping all to yourself. Stitch matching towel hangers, coaster sets, magnets, plant pokes, and more. The "Drink Milk" and "Bless Our Nest" signs will be a farm-tastic addition to any home, and don't forget the Chicken "Coopon" Box! Keep your kitchen looking farmhouse fresh with these unique, rustic designs.

Barnyard Buddies are sure to be a hit!

Leisure Arts Inc, • Maumelle Arkansas

Table of Contents

COW COASTER SET

COLOR KEY

- black - 28 yds
- white - 28 yds
- peach - 36 yds

COW COASTER SET

Coaster Size: 5½"w x 4¼"h each

Caddy Size: 4½"w x 1¾"h x 1¼"d

Supplies: Worsted weight yarn (refer to color key), two 10½" x 13½" sheets of 7 mesh plastic canvas, #16 tapestry needle, felt or cork (optional), and clear-drying craft glue (optional)

Stitches Used: Gobelin Stitch, Overcast Stitch, Tent Stitch

Instructions:

1. Follow charts and use required stitches to work Cow Coaster Set pieces.

2. Use peach yarn for all joining. To assemble Caddy, join Front and Back pieces to Sides along unworked edges. Join Bottom to Front, Back, and Sides.

3. If Coaster backing is desired, cut cork or felt slightly smaller than Coasters and glue to wrong side of the completed stitched pieces.

Caddy Side
(9 x 12 threads) (Stitch 2)

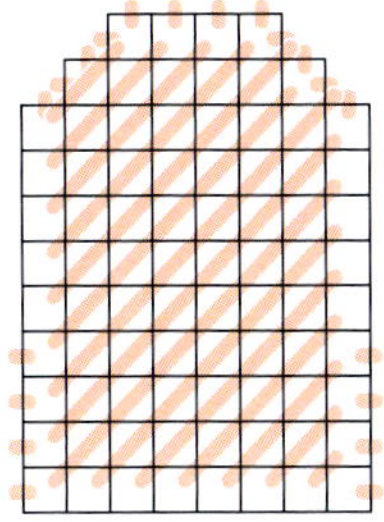

Caddy Bottom (30 x 9 threads)

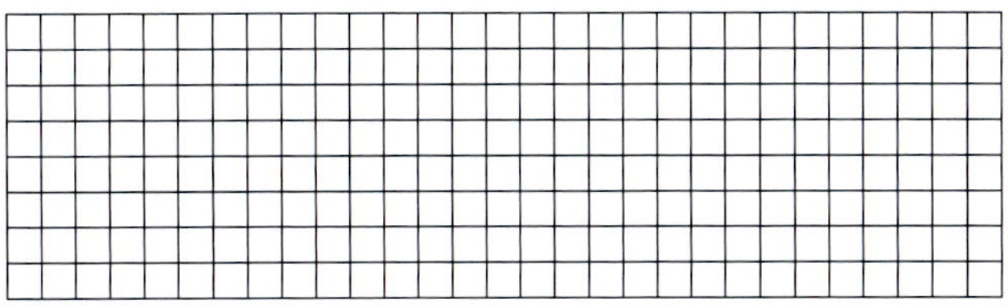

Caddy Front/Back (30 x 12 threads) (Stitch 2)

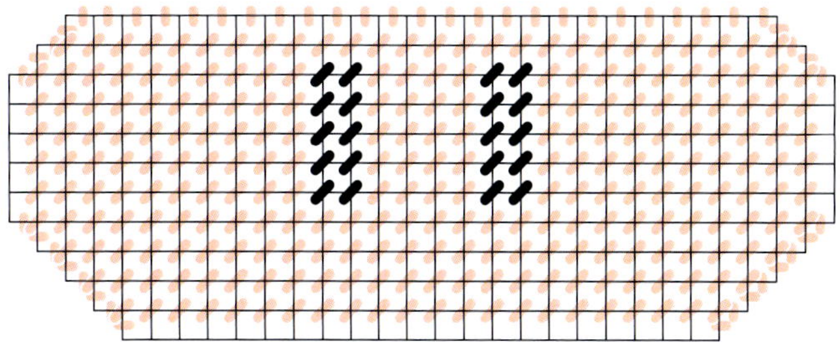

Coaster (36 x 28 threads) (Stitch 4)

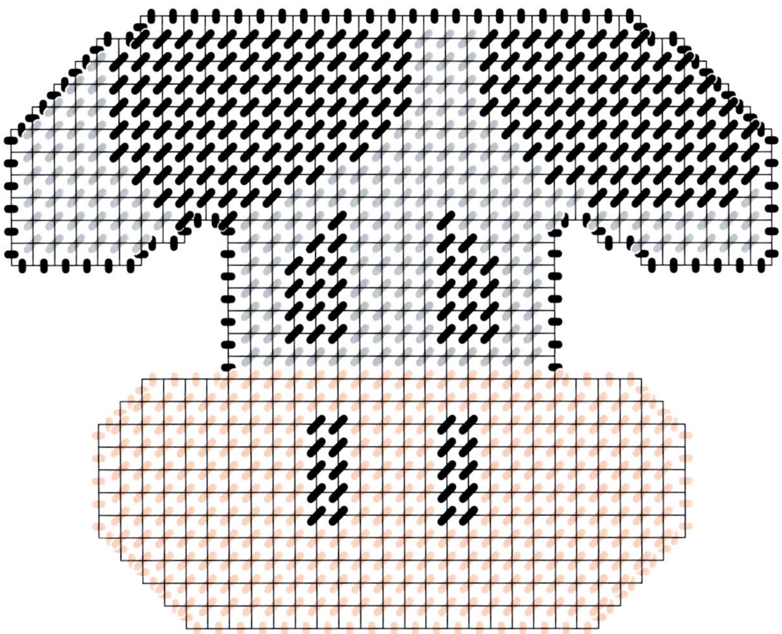

PIG NOTEPAD HOLDER

COLOR KEY

- *black - 1 yd
- pink - 12 yds
- blue - 7 yds
- white - 6 yds

*Use 2 plies of yarn for Backstitch.

PIG NOTEPAD HOLDER

Size: 4"w x 7¾"h x ½"d

Supplies: Worsted weight yarn (refer to color key), one 10½" x 13½" sheet of 7 mesh plastic canvas, #16 tapestry needle, sawtooth hanger, 3"w x 3"h notepad, pencil, and clear-drying craft glue

Stitches Used: Backstitch, Gobelin Stitch, Overcast Stitch, Tent Stitch

Instructions:

1. Follow charts and use required stitches to work Pig Notepad Holder pieces.

2. Matching ♥'s and ▼'s, join Ear A and Ear B to Front using pink yarn.

3. Refer to photo for placement and tack Nose to Front using pink yarn.

4. Refer to photo for yarn color used and join Front to Back.

5. Bend Pencil Holder in half and work through all thicknesses to tack Pencil Holder to Front and Back using white yarn.

6. Glue sawtooth hanger to wrong side of completed stitched piece.

Ear A
(8 x 12 threads)

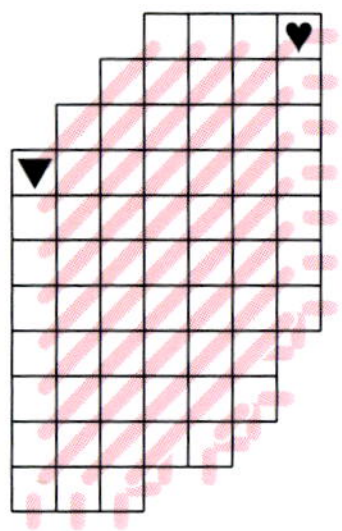

Ear B
(8 x 12 threads)

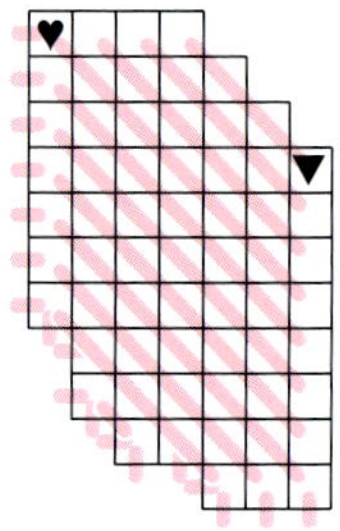

Front (26 x 46 threads)

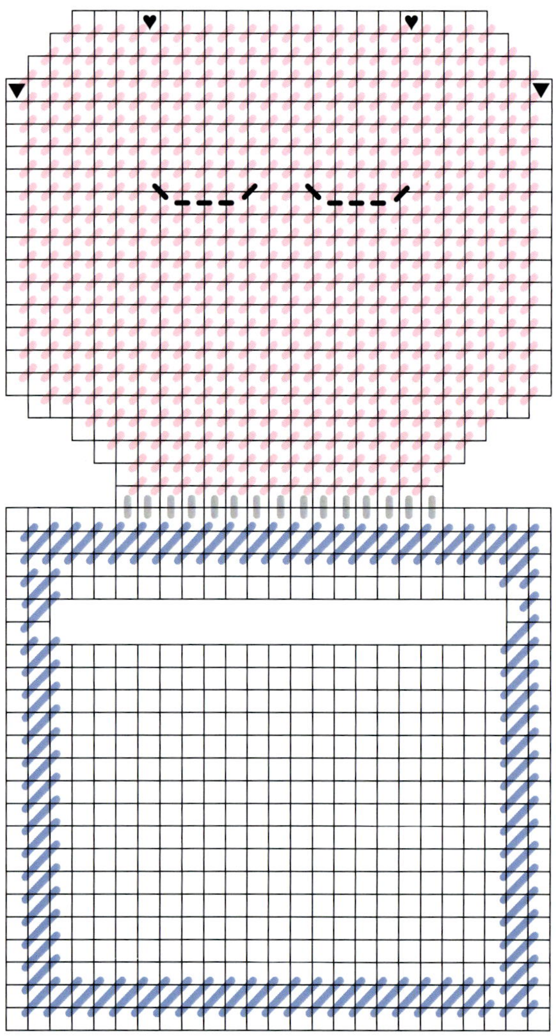

Nose
(11 x 10 threads)

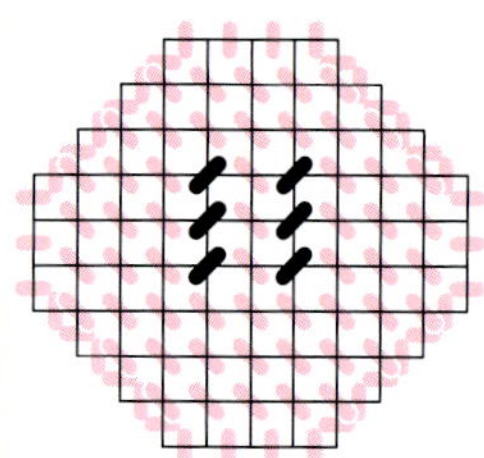

Pencil Holder
(6 x 13 threads)

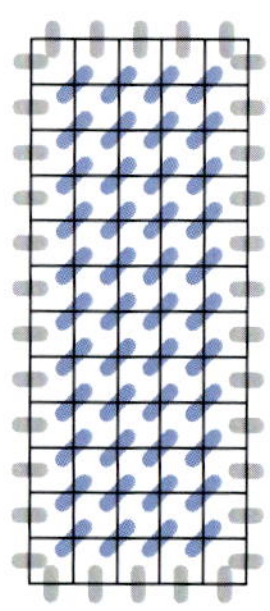

Back (26 x 46 threads)

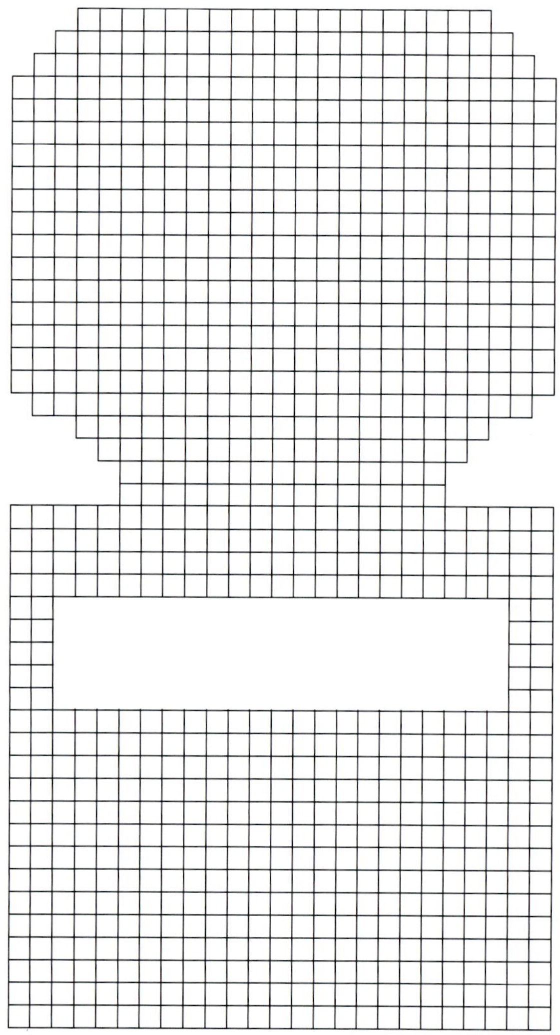

PIG TOWEL HANGER

COLOR KEY

- black - 1 yd*
- pink - 10 yds

*Use 2 plies of yarn for Backstitch.

PIG TOWEL HANGER

Size: 4"w x 5"h x 1"d

Supplies: Worsted weight yarn (refer to color key), #16 tapestry needle, one 10½" x 13½" sheet of 7 mesh plastic canvas, 3" dia gold craft ring, ¾"w Velcro® brand fastener, sewing needle, and thread

Stitches Used: Backstitch, Gobelin Stitch, Overcast Stitch, Tent Stitch

Instructions:

1. Follow charts and used required stitches to work Pig Towel Hanger pieces.

2. Join pieces using pink yarn. Matching ♥'s and ▼'s, join Ear A and Ear B to Front.

3. Refer to photo for placement and tack Nose to Front.

4. For Hanger, cut a piece of plastic canvas 6 x 36 threads. *(**Note:** Hanger is not worked.)* Stitch a 1½" piece of hook (hard) Velcro® fastener to one end of Hanger using sewing needle and thread. Stitch a 1½" piece of loop (soft) Velcro® fastener to opposite end of Hanger using sewing needle and thread. Tack center of Hanger to center of Back.

5. Insert ring between Front and Back.

6. Refer to photo for color used and join Front to Back.

Nose
(11 x 10 threads)

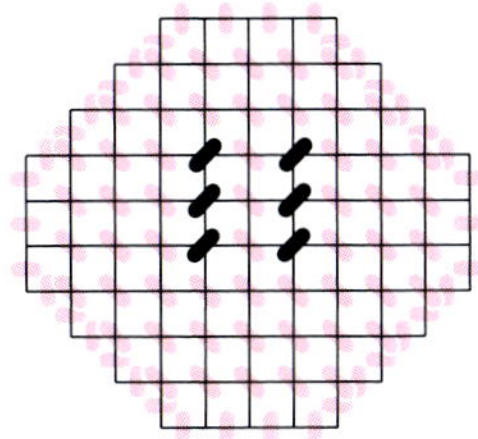

Front/Back (26 x 23 threads) (Cut 2, Stitch 1)

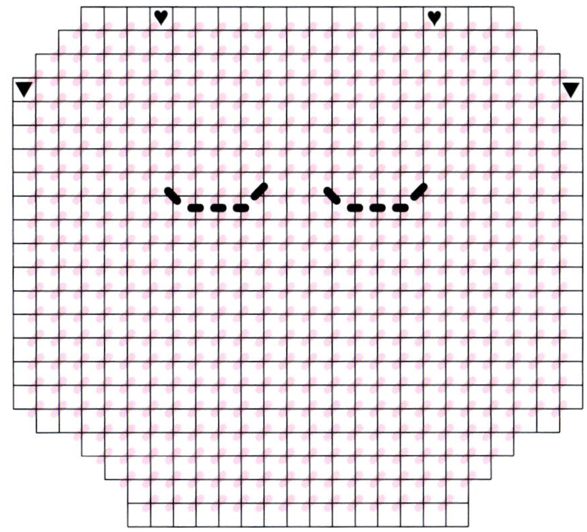

Ear A
(8 x 12 threads)

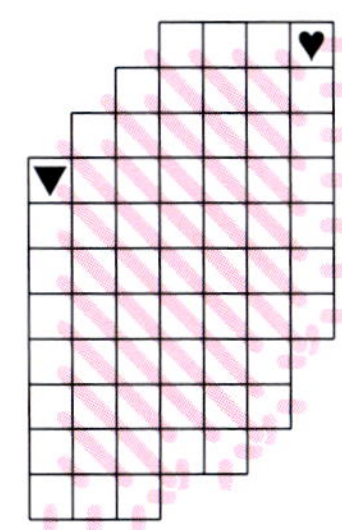

Ear B
(8 x 12 threads)

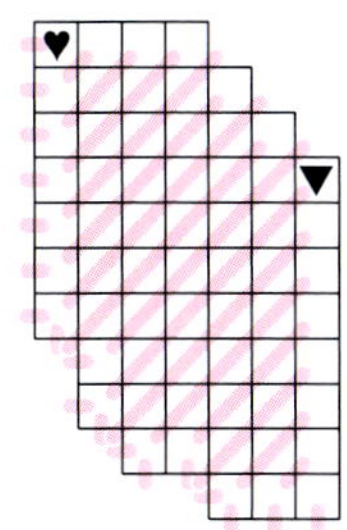

COW TOWEL HANGER

COLOR KEY

- black - 6 yds
- white - 6 yds
- peach - 7 yds

COW TOWEL HANGER

Size: 5¼"w x 6"h x ½"d

Supplies: Worsted weight yarn (refer to color key), #16 tapestry needle, one 10½" x 13½" sheet of 7 mesh plastic canvas, 3" dia gold craft ring, ¾"w Velcro® brand fastener, sewing needle, and thread

Stitches Used: Overcast Stitch, Tent Stitch

Instructions:

1. Follow chart and use required stitches to work Cow Towel Hanger.

2. For Hanger, cut a piece of plastic canvas 6 x 36 threads. *(**Note:** Hanger is not worked.)* Stitch a 1½" piece of hook (hard) Velcro® fastener to one end of Hanger using sewing needle and thread. Stitch a 1½" piece of loop (soft) Velcro® fastener to opposite end of Hanger using sewing needle and thread. Tack center of Hanger to center of Back.

3. Insert ring between Front and Back.

4. Refer to photo for color used and join Front to Back.

Front/Back (36 x 28 threads) (Cut 2, Stitch 1)

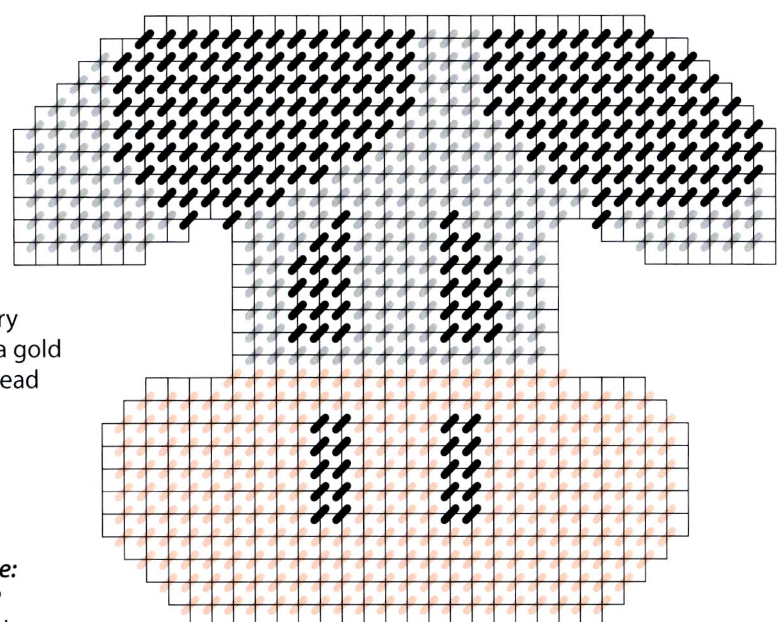

COW RECIPE CARD HOLDER

COLOR KEY
- black - 3 yds
- white - 4 yds
- peach - 3 yds

COW RECIPE CARD HOLDER

Size: 4½"w x 4½"h x 1½"d

Supplies: Worsted weight yarn (refer to color key), one 10½" x 13½" sheet of 7 mesh plastic canvas, #16 tapestry needle, wooden clothespin, black chenille stem, and clear-drying craft glue

Stitches Used: Gobelin Stitch, Overcast Stitch, Tent Stitch

Instructions:

1. Follow charts and use required stitches to work Cow Recipe Card Holder pieces.

2. Join pieces using black yarn. Matching ★'s and ■'s, join Arm to Body.

3. Matching ♥'s and ✚'s, join Leg to Body.

4. Refer to photo for placement; glue chenille stem to Body.

5. Glue clothespin to wrong side of complete stitched piece.

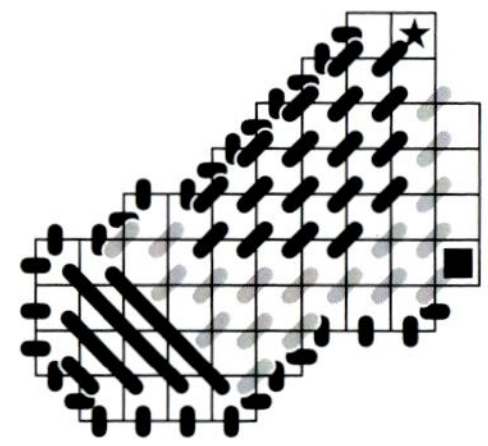

Arm (11 x 10 threads)

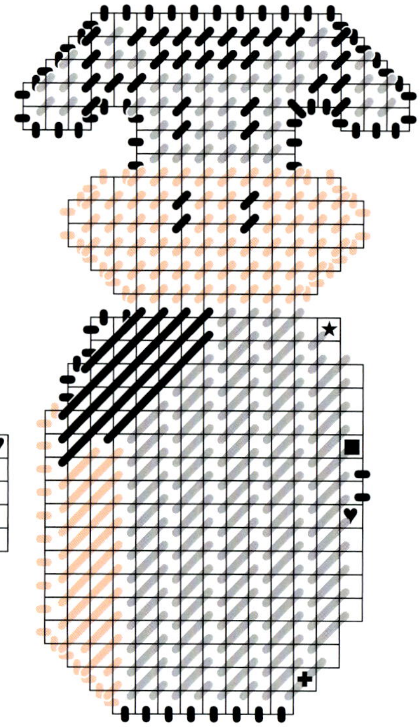

Body (18 x 31 threads)

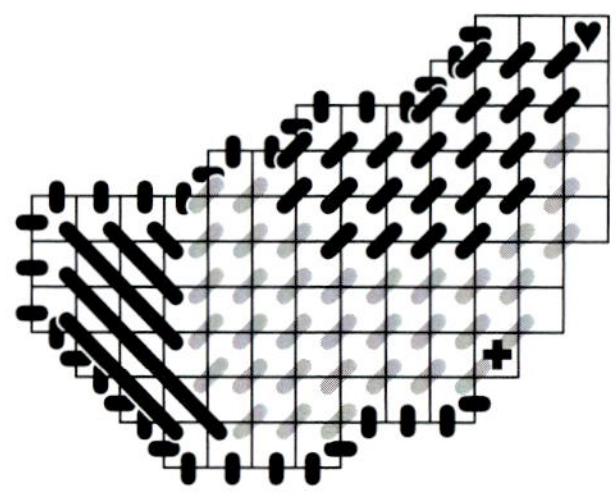

Leg (14 x 11 threads)

COW MAGNET

COLOR KEY
- black - 1 yd
- white - 1 yd
- peach - 2 yds

COW MAGNET

Size: 2⅝"w x 2"h

Supplies: Worsted weight yarn (refer to color key), one 10½" x 13½" sheet of 7 mesh plastic canvas, #16 tapestry needle, clear-drying craft glue, and magnetic strip

Stitches Used: Overcast Stitch, Tent Stitch

Instructions:

1. Follow chart and use required stitches to work Cow Magnet.

2. Glue magnetic strip to wrong side of completed stitched piece.

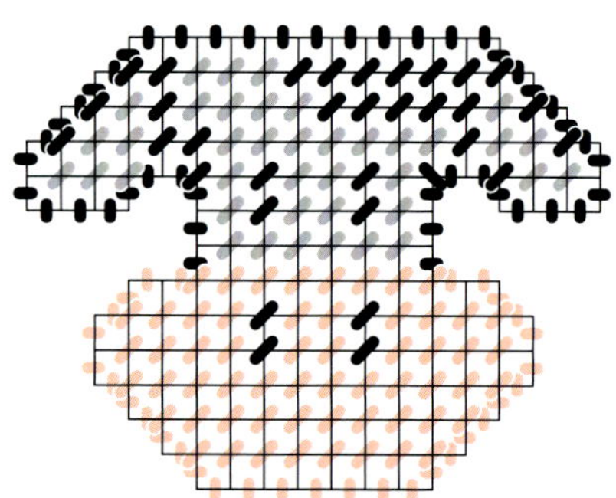

Cow Magnet (18 x 14 threads)

"DRINK MILK" SIGN

COLOR KEY

- black - 12 yds
- red - 1 yd
- grey - 4 yds
- white - 17 yds
- peach - 8 yds

DMC COLOR

- *310 - black - 2 yds

* Use 4 strands of floss for Backstitch on Bottle.

"DRINK MILK" SIGN

Size: 6¼"w x 7¾"h

Supplies: Worsted weight yarn (refer to color key), DMC Embroidery Floss (refer to color key), one 10½" x 13½" sheet of 7 mesh plastic canvas, #16 tapestry needle, 12" of ¼"w blue ribbon, black chenille stem, sawtooth hanger, and clear-drying craft glue

Stitches Used: Backstitch, Gobelin Stitch, Overcast Stitch, Tent Stitch

Instructions:

1. Follow charts and use required stitches to work "Drink Milk" Sign pieces.

2. Join pieces using black yarn. Matching ★'s and ■'s, join Arm to Body.

3. Matching ♥'s and ✚'s, join Leg to Body.

4. Refer to photo for placement and tack Milk Bottle to Body using white yarn. Tack Heart to Milk Bottle using red yarn.

5. Tie ribbon into a bow around Milk Bottle. Trim ends of ribbon.

6. Glue chenille stem to wrong side of Body.

7. Glue sawtooth hanger to wrong side of completed stitched piece.

Body (28 x 49 threads)

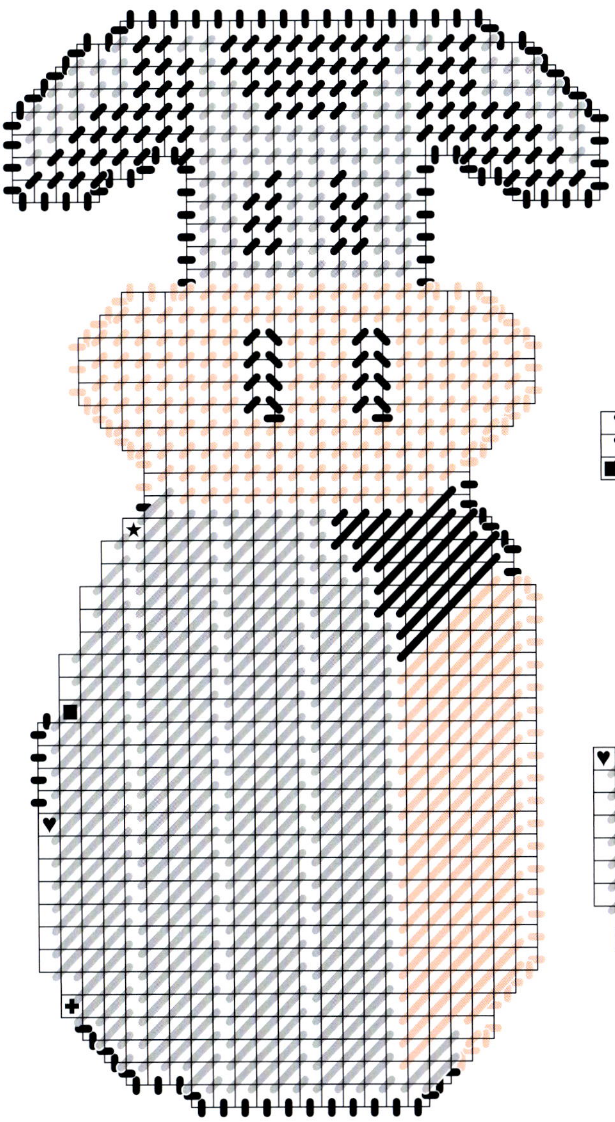

Heart (8 x 7 threads)

Arm (19 x 16 threads)

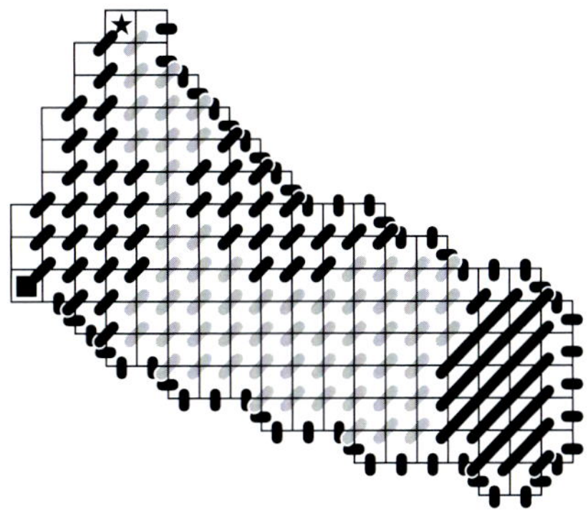

Leg (21 x 16 threads)

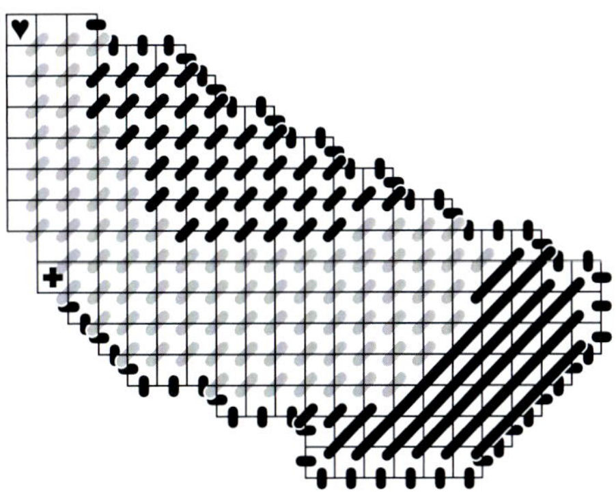

Milk Bottle (15 x 32 threads)

PIG TISSUE BOX COVER

COLOR KEY
- *black - 8 yds
- pink - 55 yds
- blue - 4 yds

*Use 2 plies of yarn for Backstitch.

Face (32 x 28 threads)

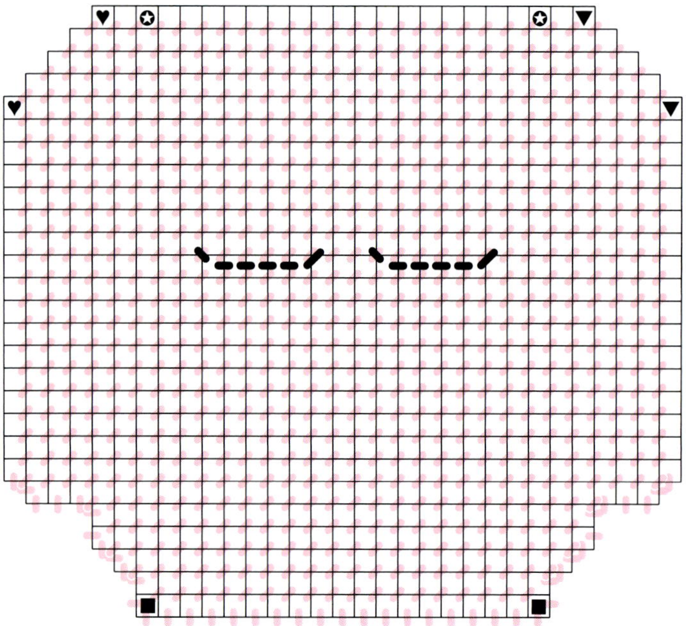

Nose (14 x 13 threads)

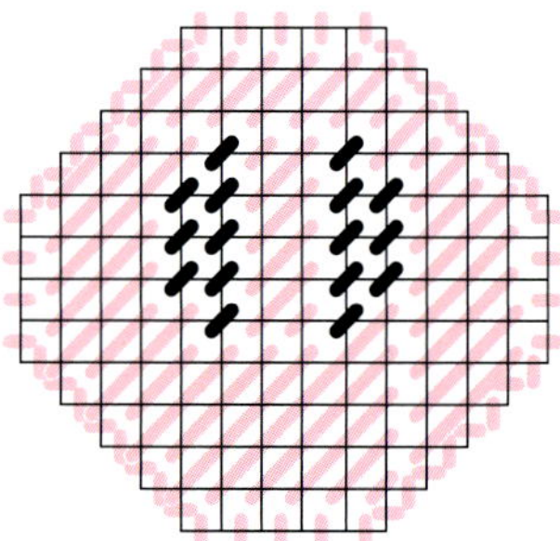

Ear A
(10 x 15 threads)

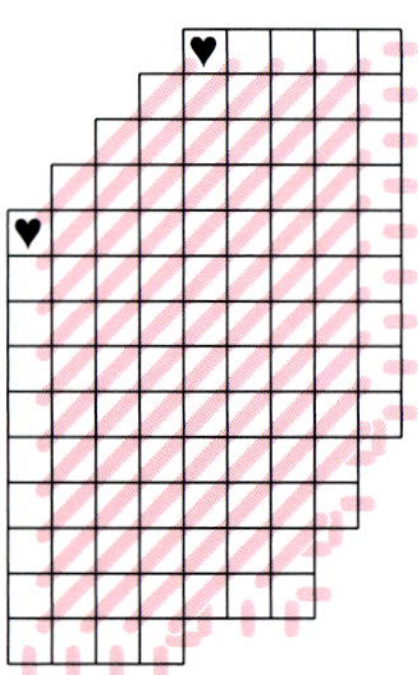

Ear B
(10 x 15 threads)

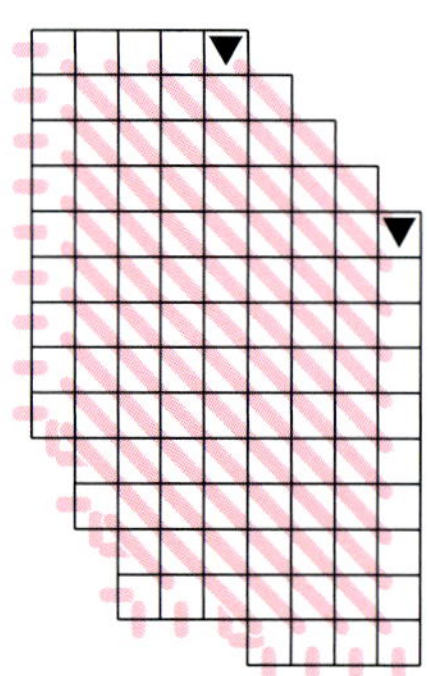

PIG TISSUE BOX COVER

Size: 4¾"w x 7"h x 4¾"d

*(**Note:** Fits a 4½"w x 5¼"h x 4½"d boutique tissue box.)*

Supplies: Worsted weight yarn (refer to color key), two 10½" x 13½" sheets of 7 mesh plastic canvas, 7" of white cloth-covered floral wire, and #16 tapestry needle

Stitches Used: Backstitch, Gobelin Stitch, Overcast Stitch, Scotch Stitch, Tent Stitch

Instructions:

1. Follow charts and use required stitches to work Pig Tissue Box Cover pieces. Unless otherwise indicated, join pieces using pink yarn.

2. Matching ♥'s and ▼'s, join Ear A and Ear B to Face.

3. Refer to photo for placement and tack Nose to Face.

4. Match ✪'s and ■'s to place Face on Front. Join Front to Sides using yarn color to match closest stitching area and working through all thicknesses.

5. Match ▲'s and ★'s to place Heart on Back. Join Back to Sides using yarn color to match closest stitching area and working through all thicknesses.

6. Join Top to Front, Back, and Sides, working through all thicknesses.

7. Insert floral wire under stitches on wrong side of Tail. Wrap Tail around index finger to form a spiral, leaving last ½" straight.

8. Tack straight end of Tail to Back at ♦.

Front (32 x 38 threads)

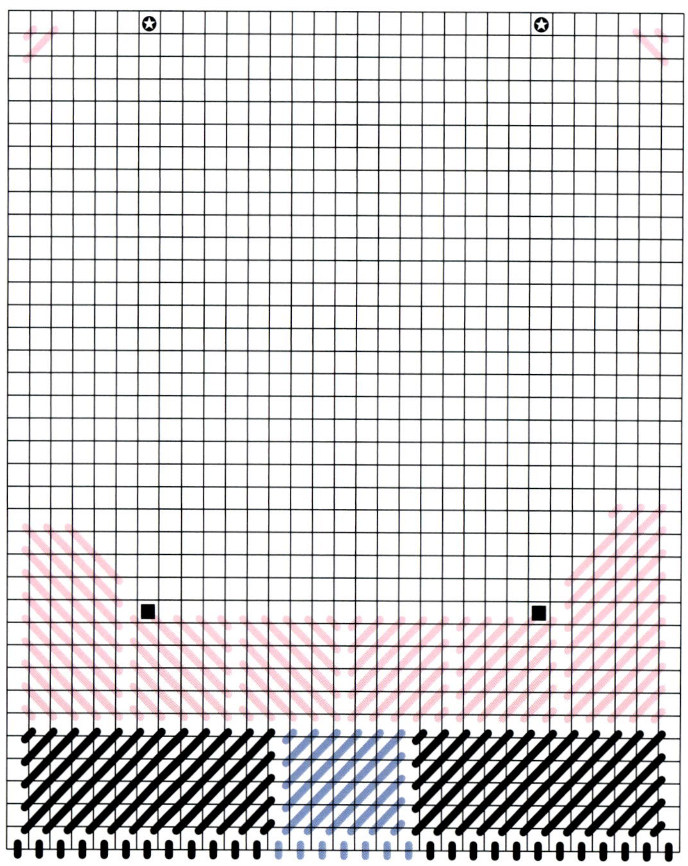

Tail (46 x 4 threads)

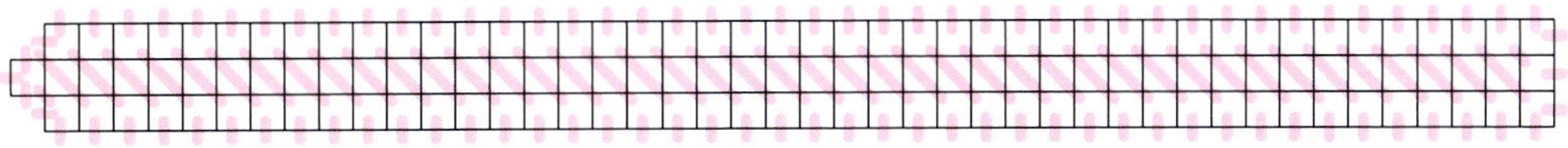

Heart (32 x 33 threads)

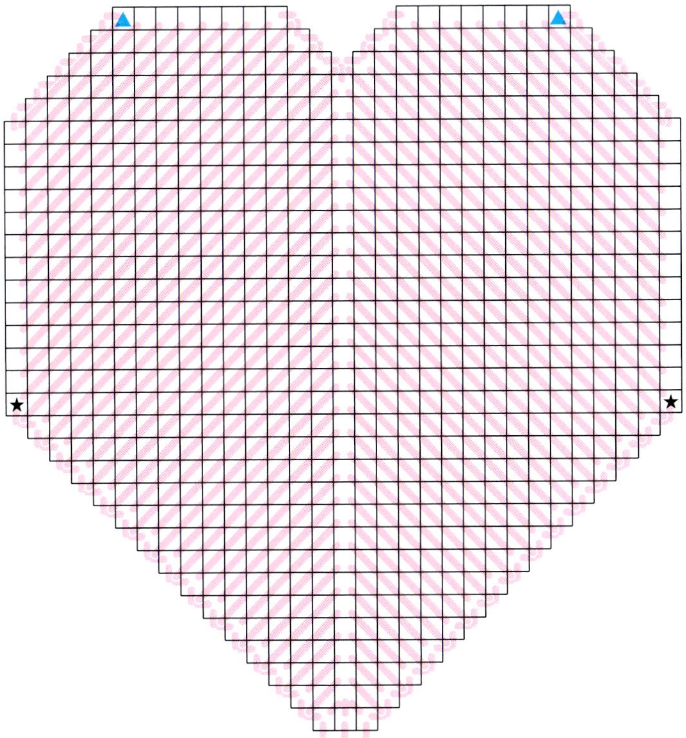

Top (32 x 32 threads)

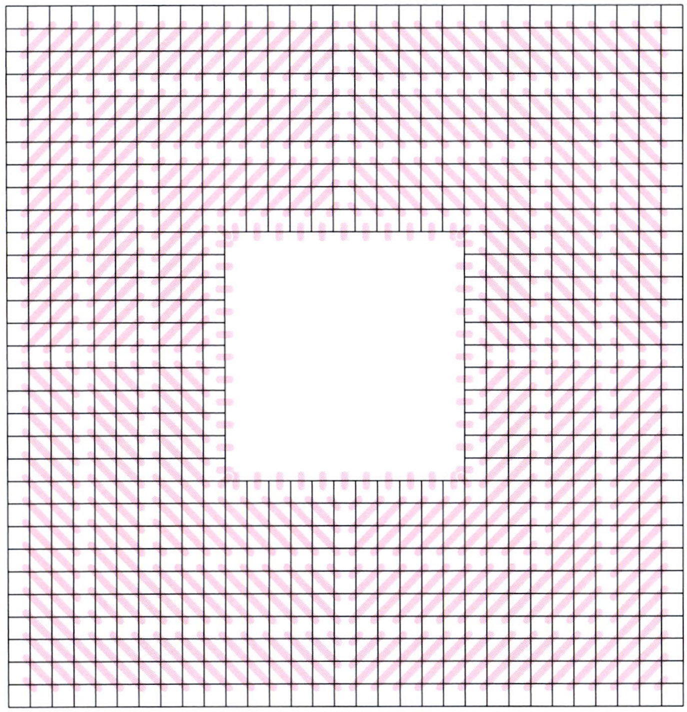

Back (32 x 38 threads)

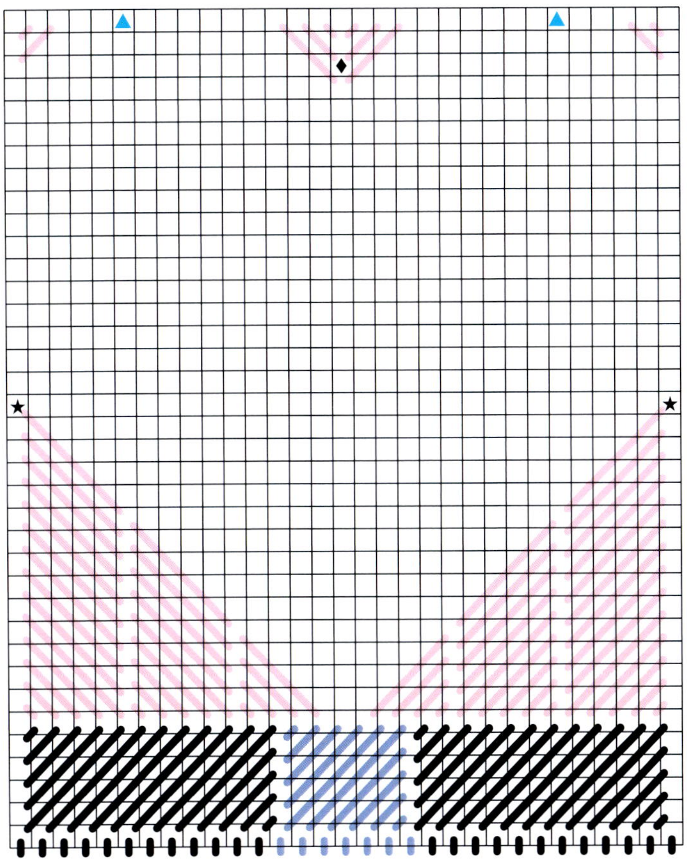

Side (32 x 38 threads) (Stitch 2)

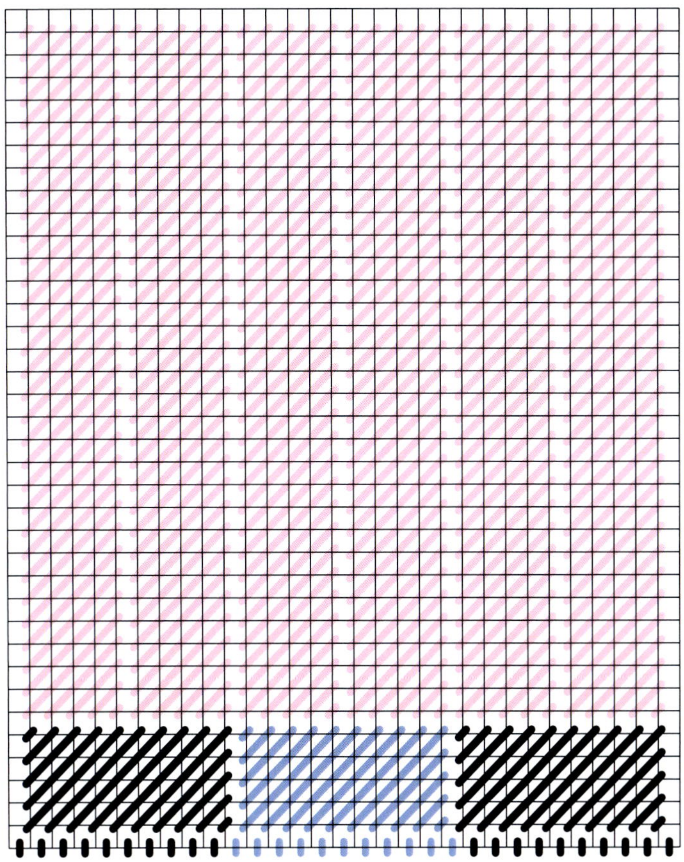

"PORK AND VINES"

COLOR KEY

- *black - 2 yds
- red - 15 yds
- pink - 5 yds
- gold - 2 yds
- white - 15 yds
- *black Fr. Knot

*Use 2 plies of yarn.

Heart
(8 x 7 threads)

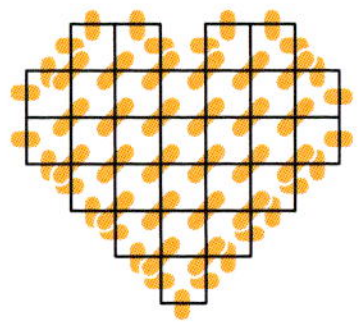

Ear A
(5 x 6 threads)

Ear B
(5 x 6 threads)

Face
(13 x 13 threads)

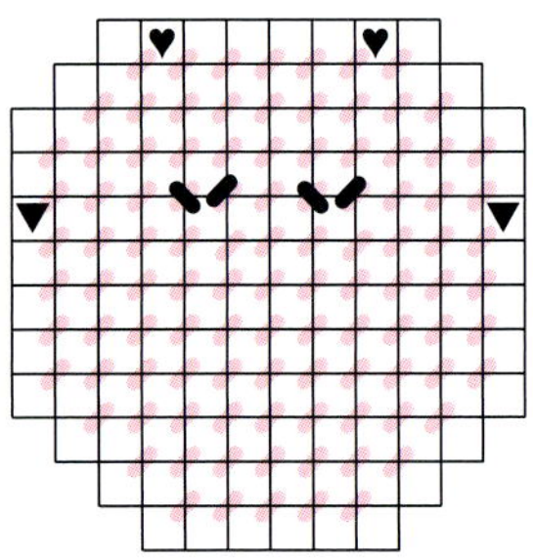

Nose
(5 x 5 threads)

"PORK AND VINE" (shown on page 20)

Can Cover Size: 4¼"h x 3"dia

Approx. Plant Poke Size: 1⅞"w x 5¼"h

Supplies: Worsted weight yarn (refer to color key), two 10½" x 13½" sheets of 7 mesh plastic canvas, #16 tapestry needle, three wooden skewers, 3" dia. can, clear-drying craft glue.

Stitches Used: Backstitch, French Knot, Goblin Stitch, Overcast Stitch, Tent Stitch

Instructions:

1. Follow charts and use required stitches to work "Pork and Vine" Can Cover and three sets of Pig pieces.

2. Refer to photo for placement and tack Heart to Can Cover using gold yarn. Wrap Can Cover around can. Join unworked edges using yarn color to match closest stitching area.

3. Matching ♥'s and ▼'s, use pink yarn to join Ear A and Ear B to Face. Refer to photo for placement and tack nose to Face using pink yarn. Glue wooden skewers to back of completed stitched pieces.

4. Refer to photo for placement and insert plant pokes into can.

PIG MAGNET

Size: 1⅞"w x 1⅞"h

Supplies: Worsted weight yarn (refer to color key), one 10½ x 13½" sheet of 7 mesh plastic canvas, #16 tapestry needle, clear-drying craft glue, and magnetic strip

Stitches Used: Backstitch, Overcast Stitch, Tent Stitch

Instructions:

1. Follow chart and use required stitches to work Pig pieces.

2. Matching ♥'s and ▼'s, join Ear A and Ear B to Face using pink yarn.

3. Refer to photo for placement and tack Nose to Face using pink yarn.

4. Glue magnetic strip to wrong side of completed stitched piece.

Can Cover (65 x 29 threads)

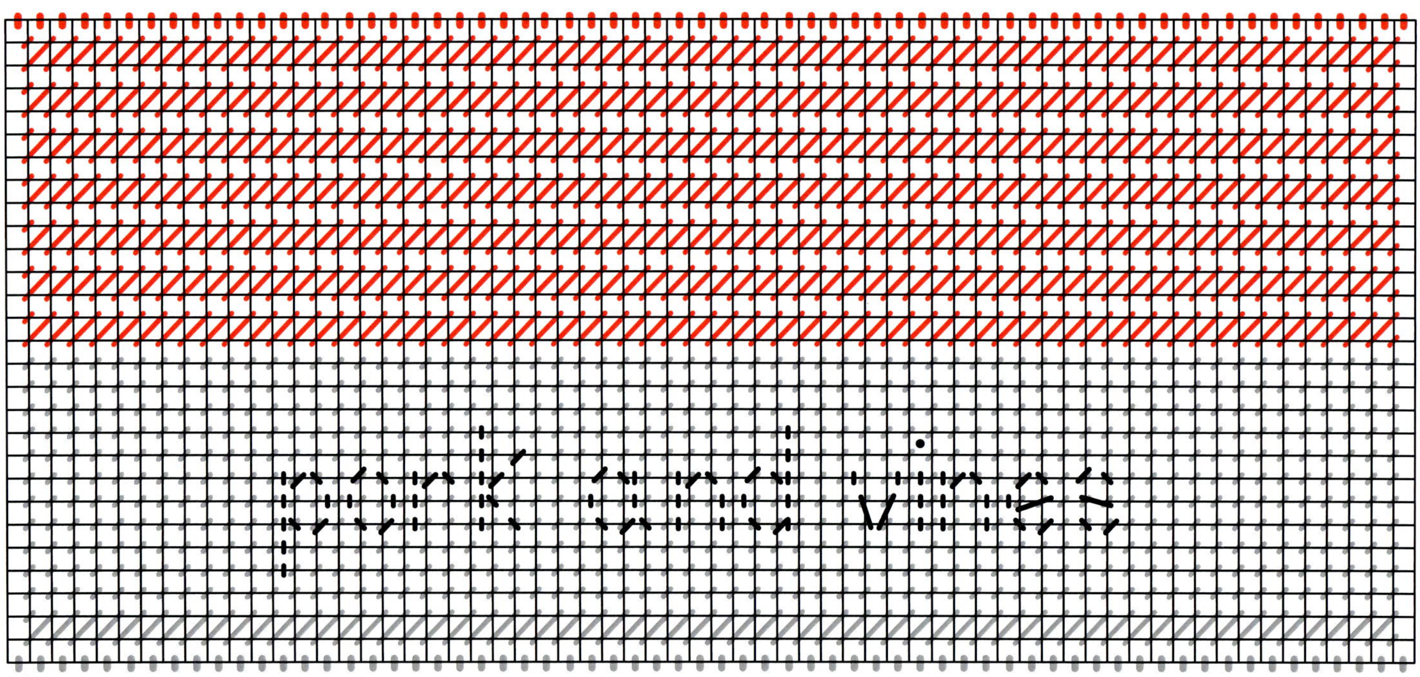

PIG COASTER SET

COLOR KEY

- *black - 3 yds
- pink - 50 yds
- blue - 1 yd

*Use 2 plies of yarn for Backstitch.

Ear A
(8 x 12 threads)

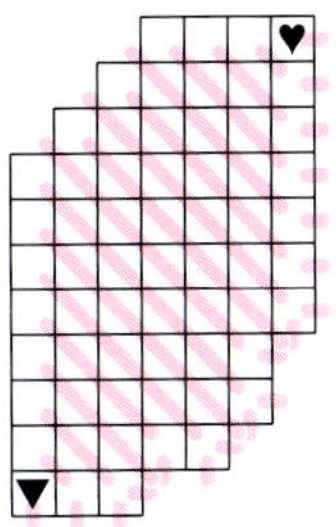

Ear B
(8 x 12 threads)

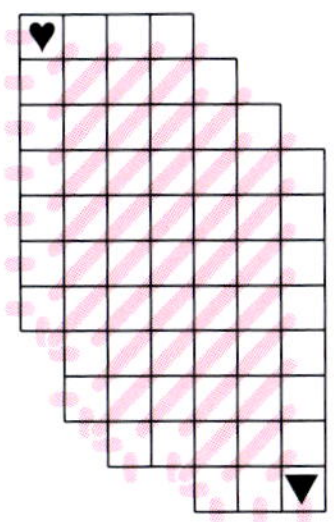

Nose
(11 x 10 threads)

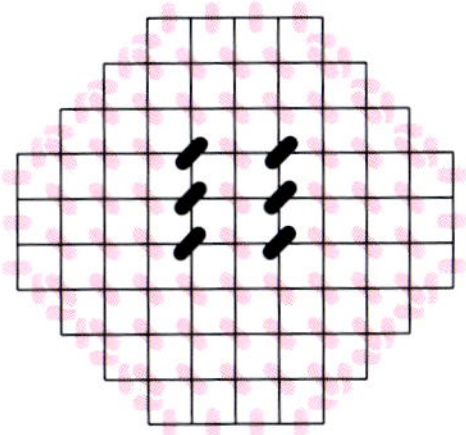

PIG COASTER SET

Coaster Size: 4¼"w x 3½"h each

Caddy Size: 4"w x 3½"h x 1¼"d

Supplies For Entire Set: Worsted weight yarn (refer to color key), two 10½" x 13½" sheets of 7 mesh plastic canvas, #16 tapestry needle, 9" of white cloth-covered floral wire, wooden skewer, felt or cork (optional), and clear-drying craft glue (optional)

Stitches Used: Backstitch, Gobelin Stitch, Overcast Stitch, Tent Stitch

Instructions:

1. Follow charts and use required stitches to work Pig Coaster Set pieces. Unless otherwise indicated, join pieces using pink yarn.

2. Matching ♥'s and ▼'s, join Ear A and Ear B to Caddy Front.

3. Refer to photo for placement and tack Nose to Caddy Front.

4. To assemble Caddy, join short edges of Sides to short edges of Bottom. Join Sides and Bottom to Back using yarn color to match closest stitching area. Join Sides and Bottom to Front. Work Overcast Stitches to cover unworked edges of Caddy using pink yarn.

5. Tightly wrap and glue floral wire with pink yarn. Wrap yarn-covered floral wire around a wooden skewer to form a spiral, leaving last ½" straight.

6. Glue straight end of Tail to Caddy Back at ♦.

7. If backing is desired for Coasters, cut cork or felt slightly smaller than Coasters and glue to wrong side of completed stitched pieces.

Caddy Back (26 x 10 threads)

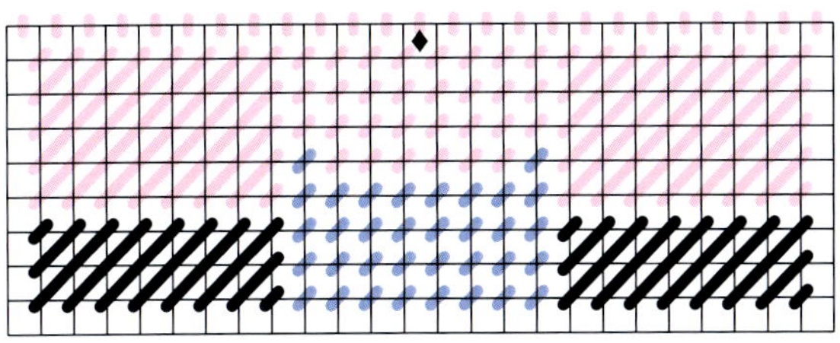

Caddy Side
(9 x 10 threads)
(Stitch 2)

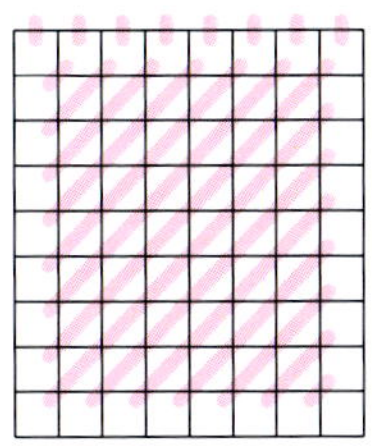

Caddy Bottom (26 x 9 threads)

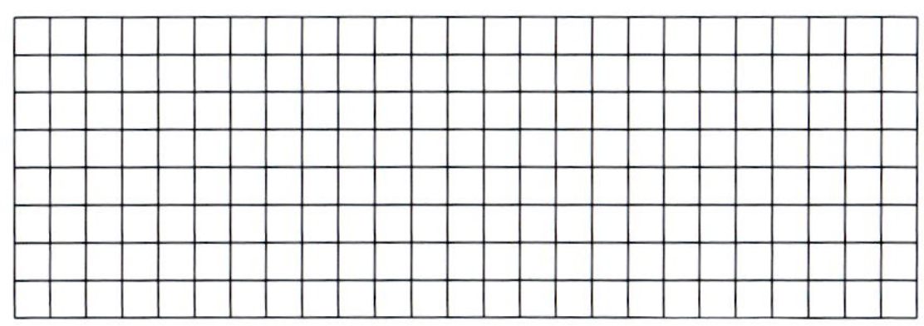

Caddy Front (26 x 23 threads)

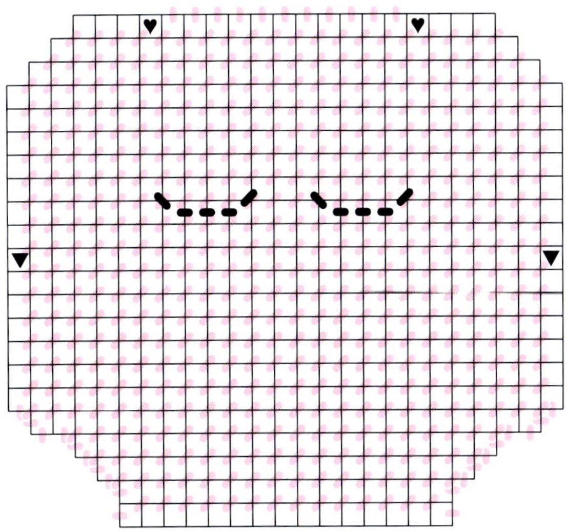

Coaster (28 x 24 threads) (Stitch 4)

PIG RECIPE CARD HOLDER

COLOR KEY
- black - 3 yds*
- pink - 11 yds
- blue - 1 yds

*Use 2 plies of yarn for Backstitch.

PIG RECIPE CARD HOLDER

Size: 3¾"w x 4¾"h x 1¼"d

Supplies: Worsted weight yarn (refer to color key), one 10½" x 13½" sheet of 7 mesh plastic canvas, #16 tapestry needle, wooden clothespin, 5" of white cloth-covered floral wire, wooden skewer, and clear-drying craft glue

Stitches Used: Backstitch, Gobelin Stitch, Overcast Stitch, Tent Stitch

Instructions:

1. Follow charts and use required stitches to work Pig Recipe Card Holder pieces.

2. Join pieces using pink yarn. Matching ♥'s and ▼'s, join Ear A and Ear B to Front.

3. Refer to photo for placement; tack nose to front.

4. Tightly wrap and glue floral wire with pink yarn. Wrap yarn-covered floral wire around wooden skewer to form a spiral, leaving last ½" straight.

5. Glue straight end of Tail to back at ♦.

6. Glue clothespin between Front and Back.

Nose (11 x 10 threads)

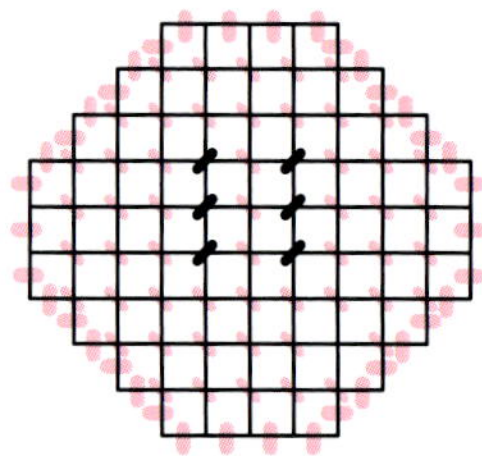

Ear A (8 x 12 threads)

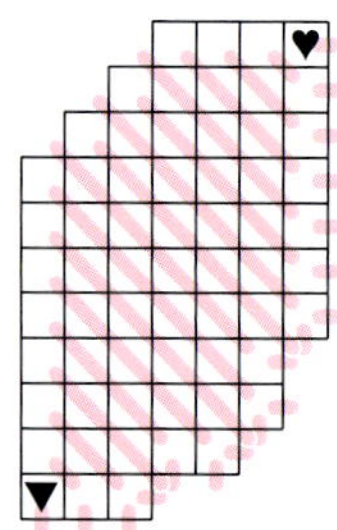

Ear B (8 x 12 threads)

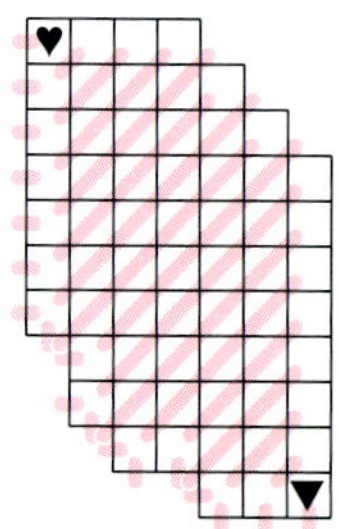

Front (26 x 23 threads)

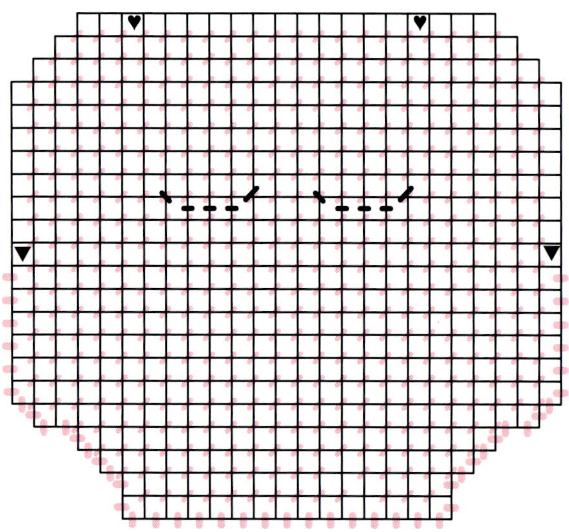

Back (26 x 23 threads)

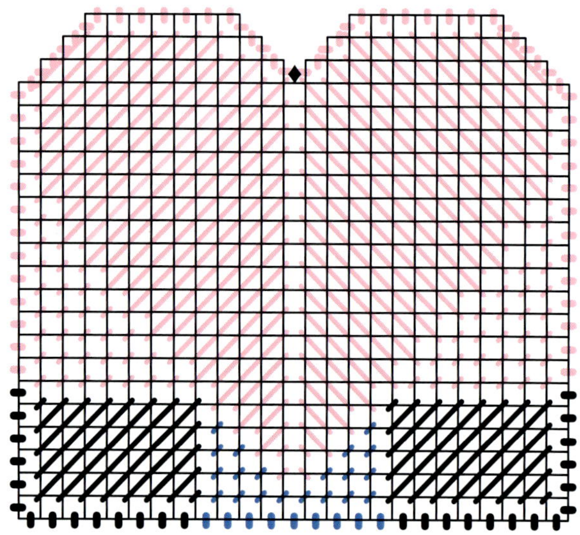

"BLESS OUR NEST" SIGN

COLOR KEY		DMC	COLOR
black - 1 yd	white - 7 yds	*blanc - white Fr. Knot - 10 yds *Use 6 strands of floss.	
red - 3 yds	dk blue - 10 yds		
tan - 1 yd	yellow - 1 yd		
blue - 25 yds	*red bst		

*Use 2 plies of yarn for Backstitch.

"Bless Our Nest" (70 x 75 threads) (Cut 2)

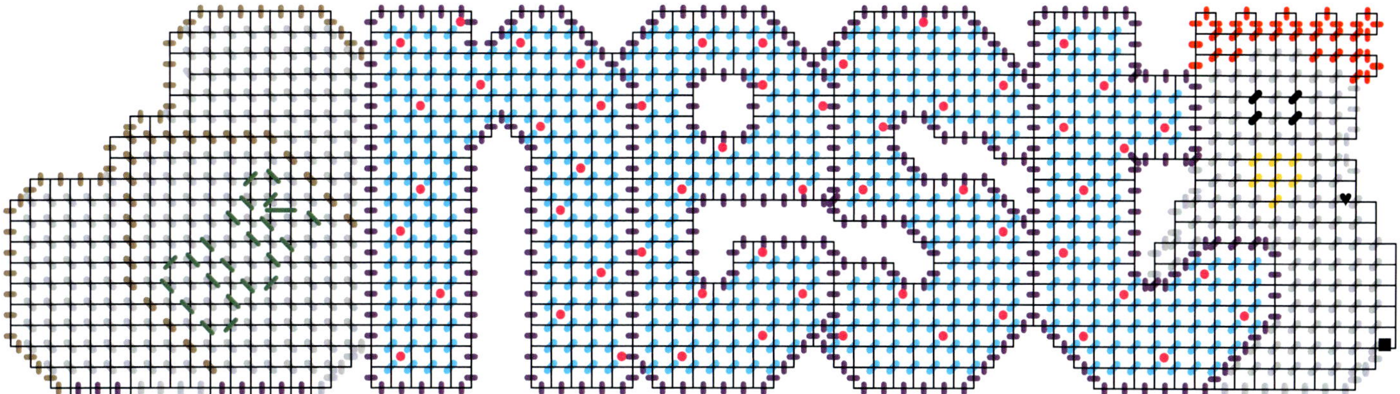

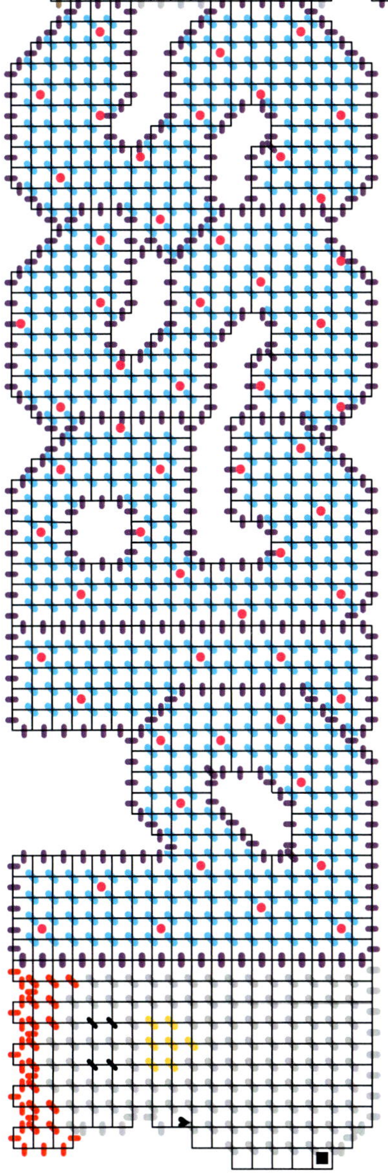

Wing A
(6 x 9 threads)

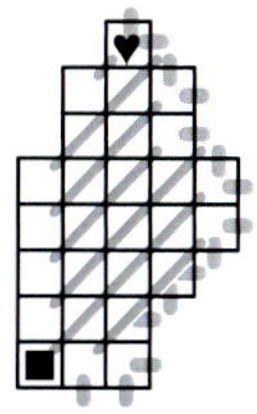

Wing B
(6 x 9 threads)

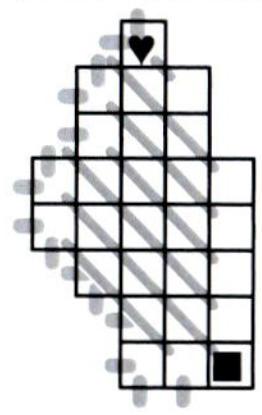

"BLESS OUR NEST' SIGN
Size: 10½"w x 11¼"h

Supplies: Worsted weight yarn (refer to color key), DMC embroidery Floss (Refer to color key) two 10½" x 13½" sheets of 7 mesh plastic canvas, and #16 tapestry needle.

Stitches Used: Backstitch, French Knot, Gobelin Stitch, Overcast Stitch, and Tent Stitch

Instructions:

1. Follow charts and use required stitches to work "Bless Our Nest" Sign pieces. Stitch "Bless Our Nest" Sign piece only through two thickness of canvas.

2. Matching ♥'s and ■'s, join Wing A and Wing B to "Bless Our Nest" using white yarn.

CHICKEN BOOKEND

COLOR KEY

black - 1 yd	
red - 4 yds	
blue - 59 yds	
white - 20 yds	
yellow - 4 yds	
DMC	**COLOR**
*blanc	white Fr. Knot - 4 yds

* Use 6 strands of floss.

Front (27 x 56 threads)

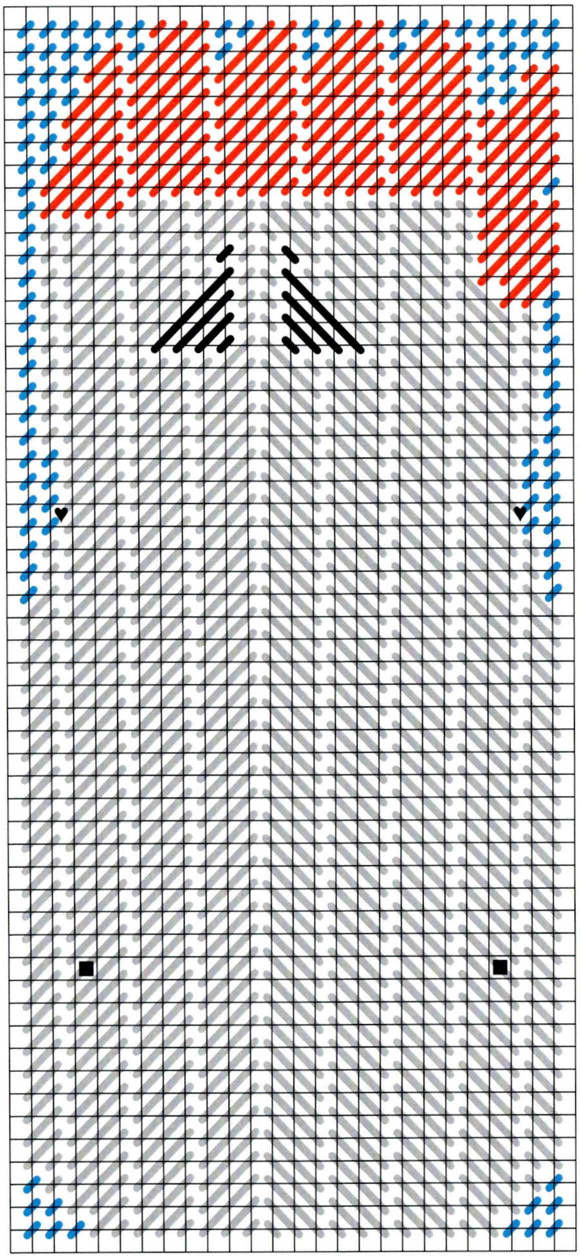

CHICKEN BOOKEND

Size: 4"w x 8½"h x 2½"d

*(**Note:** Fits a 3$\frac{5}{8}$"w x 8"h x 2$\frac{1}{8}$"d brick.)*

Supplies: Worsted weight yarn (refer to color key), DMC Embroidery Floss (refer to color key), two 10½" x 13½" sheets of 7 mesh plastic canvas, #16 tapestry needle, brick, and plastic wrap

Stitches Used: French Knot, Gobelin Stitch, Overcast Stitch, Tent Stitch

Instructions:

1. Follow charts and use required stitches to work Chicken Bookend. Unless otherwise indicated, join pieces using blue yarn.

2. Refer to photo for placement to tack Beak and Foot pieces to Front using yellow yarn.

3. Match ♥'s and ■'s to place Wing A and Wing B on Front. Join Front and Wings to Sides through all thicknesses using yarn color to match closest stitching area on Front.

4. Join Front to Sides along long edges.

5. Join Top and Bottom to Front and Sides.

6. Wrap brick with plastic wrap. Place brick inside Bookend. Join Back to Sides, Top, and Bottom.

Foot (8 x 8 threads)
(Stitch 2)

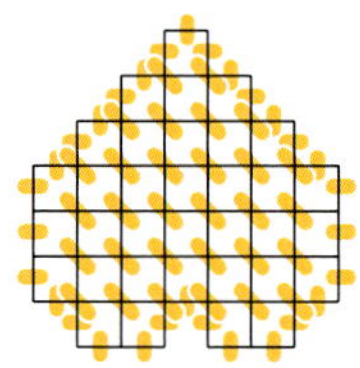

Beak (12 x 8 threads)

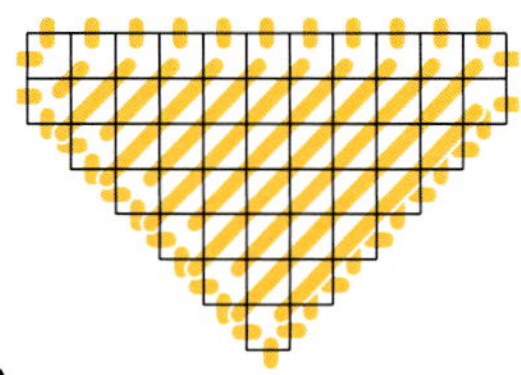

Wing A
(13 x 22 threads)

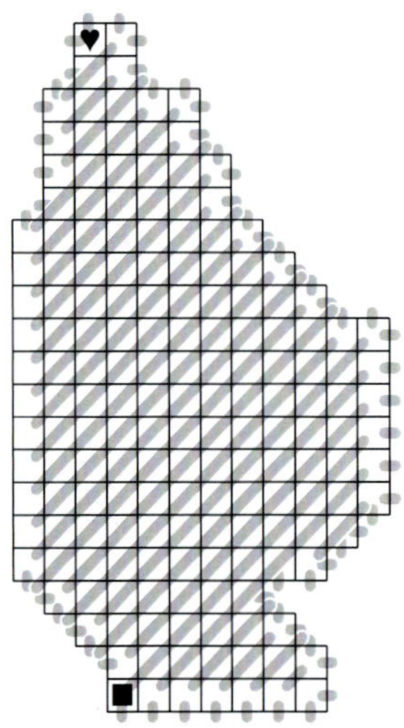

Wing B
(13 x 22 threads)

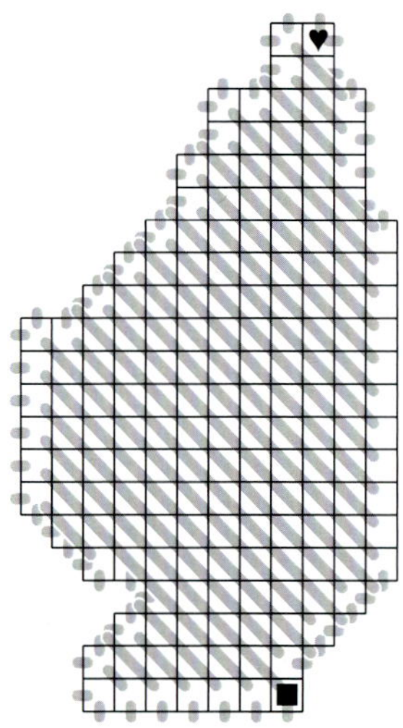

Top/Bottom (27 x 17 threads) (Stitch 2)

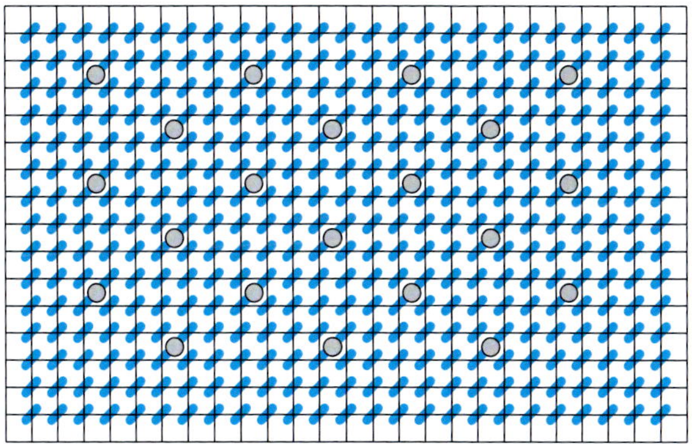

Side (17 x 56 threads) (Stitch 2)

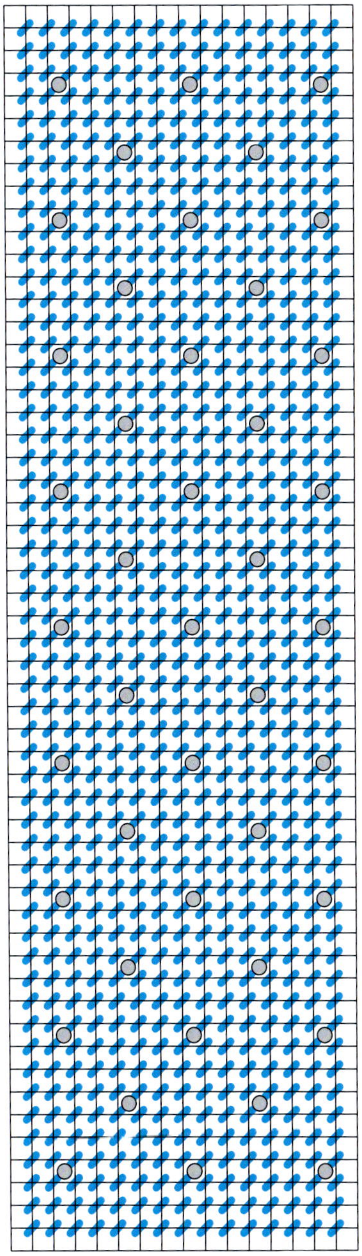

Back (27 x 56 threads)

CHICKEN CHANGE BOX

COLOR KEY	
black - 1 yd	
red - 2 yds	
blue - 39 yds	
white - 9 yds	
dk blue- 5 yds	
*yellow - 5 yds	
* Use 2 plies of yarn for Backstitch.	
DMC	COLOR
*blanc	white Fr. Knot - 5 yds
* Use 6 strands of floss.	

CHICKEN "CHANGE" BOX

Size: 7"w x 1½"h x 5½"d

Supplies: Worsted weight yarn (refer to color key), DMC Embroidery Floss (refer to color key), two 10½" x 13½" sheets of 7 mesh plastic canvas, #16 tapestry needle, felt, and clear-drying craft glue

Stitches Used: Backstitch, French Knot, Gobelin Stitch, Overcast Stitch, Tent Stitch

Instructions:

1. Follow charts and use required stitches to work Chicken Change Box pieces. Before working Backstitches and French Knots, complete background of Top with blue Tent Stitches as indicated on chart.

2. Unless otherwise indicated, use dk blue yarn for all joining. Join Top Short Sides to Top Long Side along short edges. Join Top Sides to Top.

3. Refer to photo to assemble Bottom pieces. Join Bottom Sides to Bottom Front along short edges. Join Bottom Front and Bottom Sides to Bottom.

4. Join short edges of Long Divider to Bottom Sides at ✚'s. Join Long Divider to Bottom.

5. Matching ♦'s and ◗'s, join Short Dividers to Long Divider and Bottom Front. Join Short Dividers to Bottom.

6. Join Back to Top, Bottom, and Bottom Sides. Work Overcast Stitches to cover unworked edges of Top Short Sides of Chicken Change Box using dark blue yarn.

7. Matching ♥'s and ■'s, join Wing A and Wing B to Chicken using white yarn. Tack Chicken to Change Box using white yarn.

8. Glue felt inside top and inside Bottom. Glue felt on Bottom.

Top Short Side (37 x 7 threads) (stitch 2)

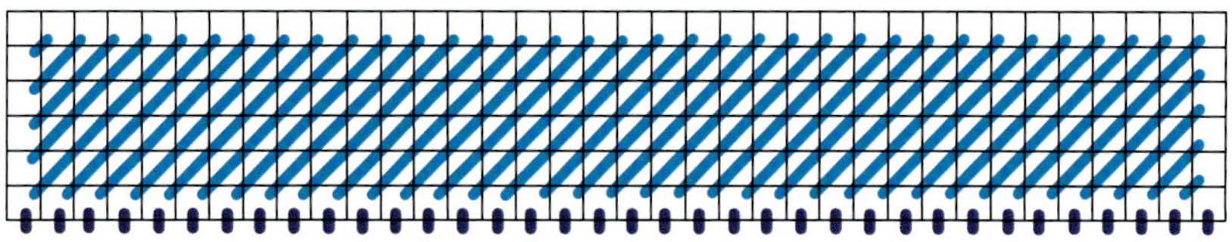

Top (46 x 37 threads)

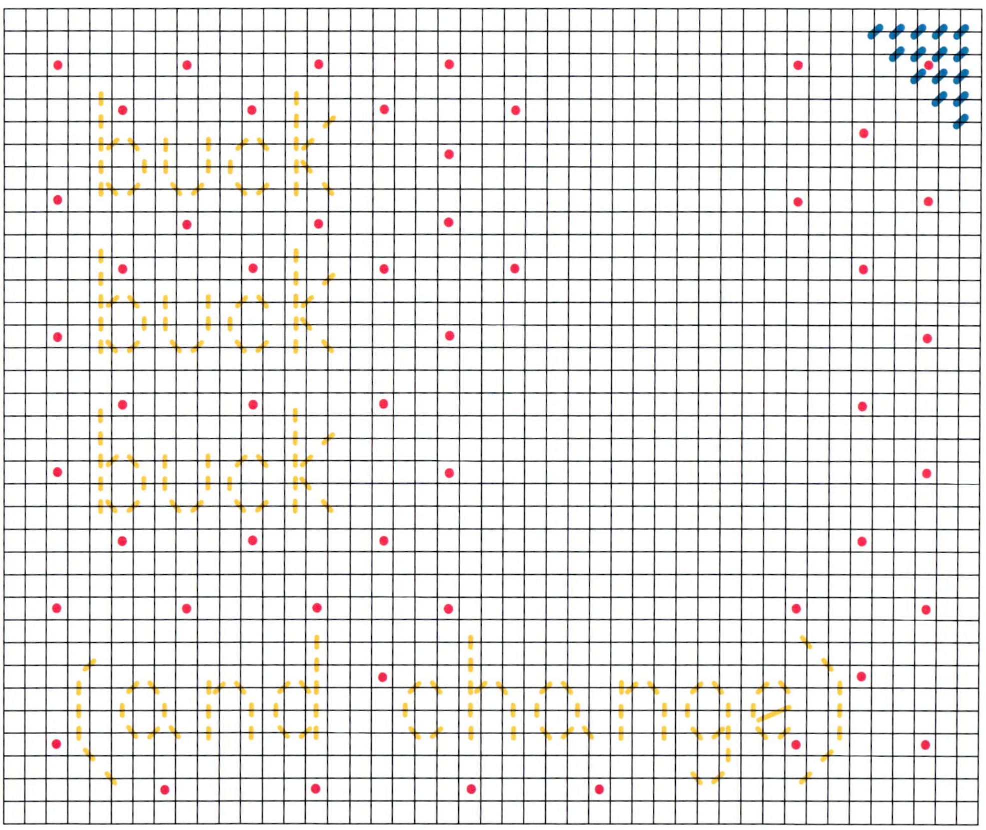

Short Divider
(17 x 7 threads) (Cut 2)

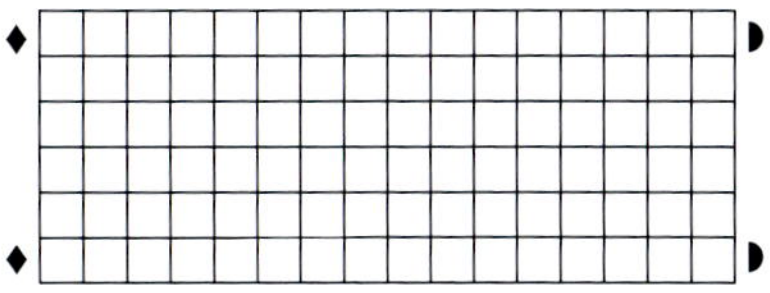

Top Long Side
(46 x 7 threads)

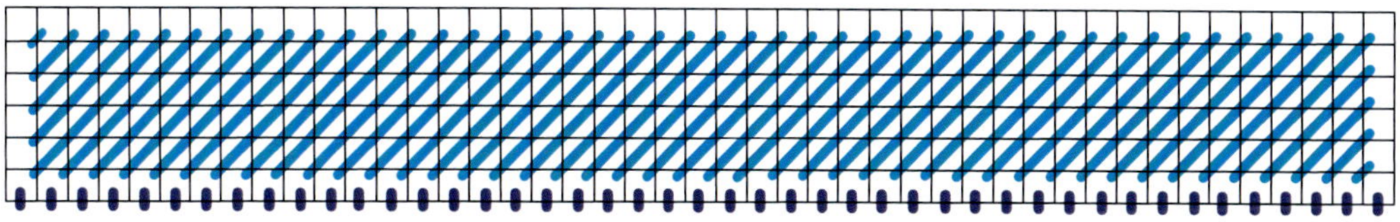

Wing A
(8 x 15 threads)

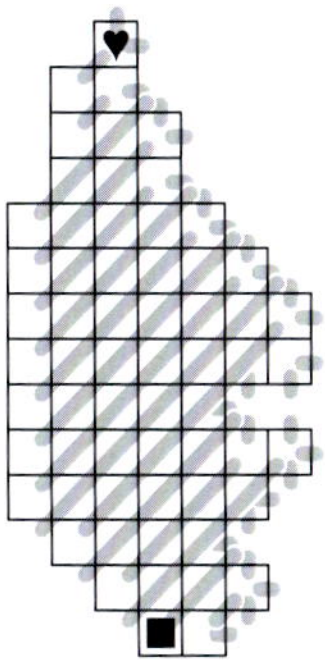

Wing B
(8 x 15 threads)

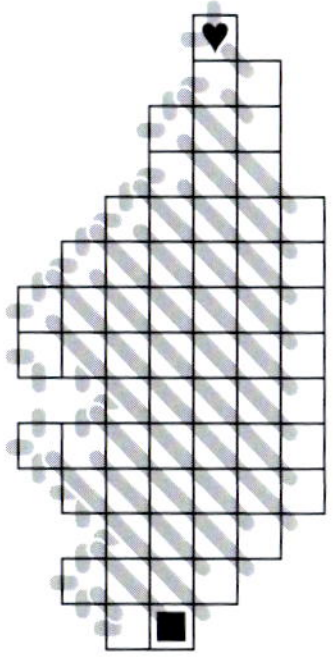

Bottom Side (36 x 7 threads) (Cut 2)

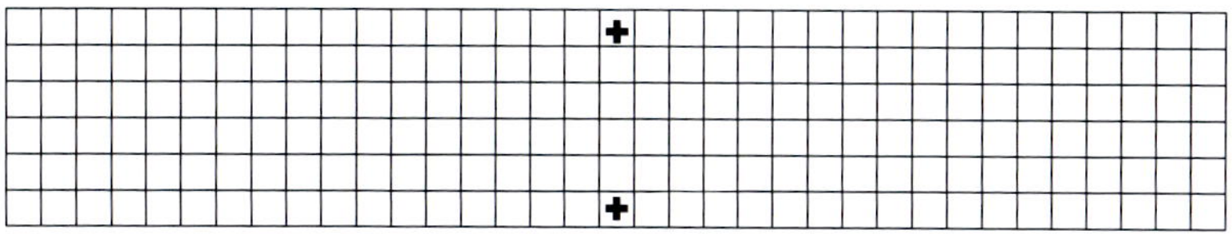

Back (44 x 7 threads)

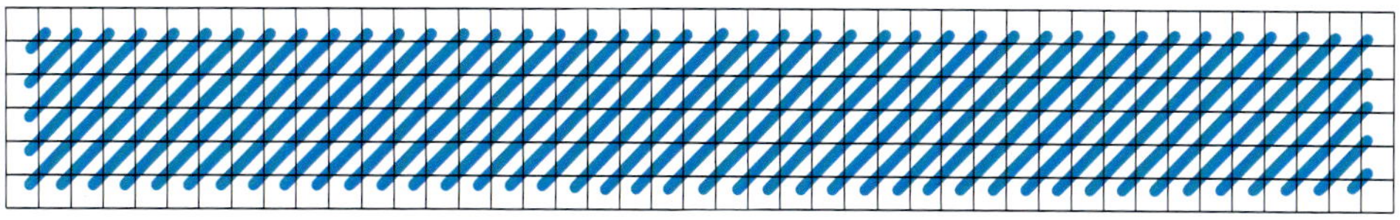

Chicken (16 x 28 threads)

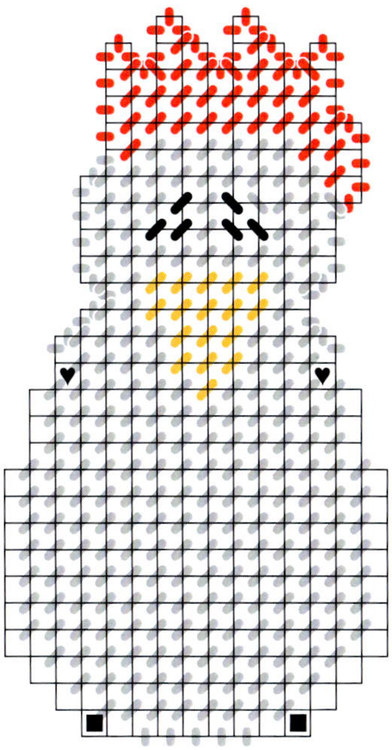

Bottom Front/Long Divider (44 x 7 threads) (Cut 2)

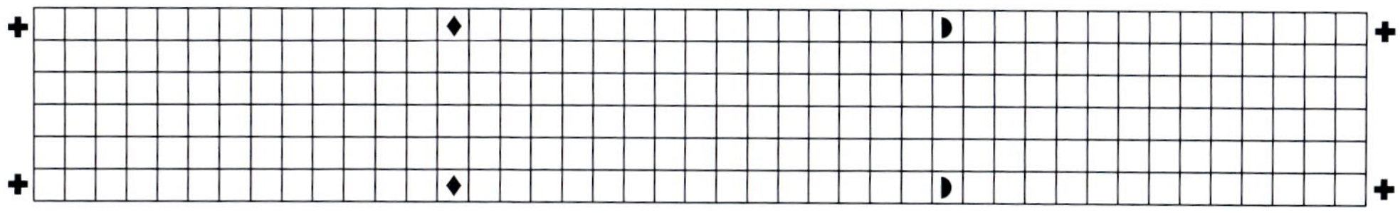

Bottom (44 x 36 threads)

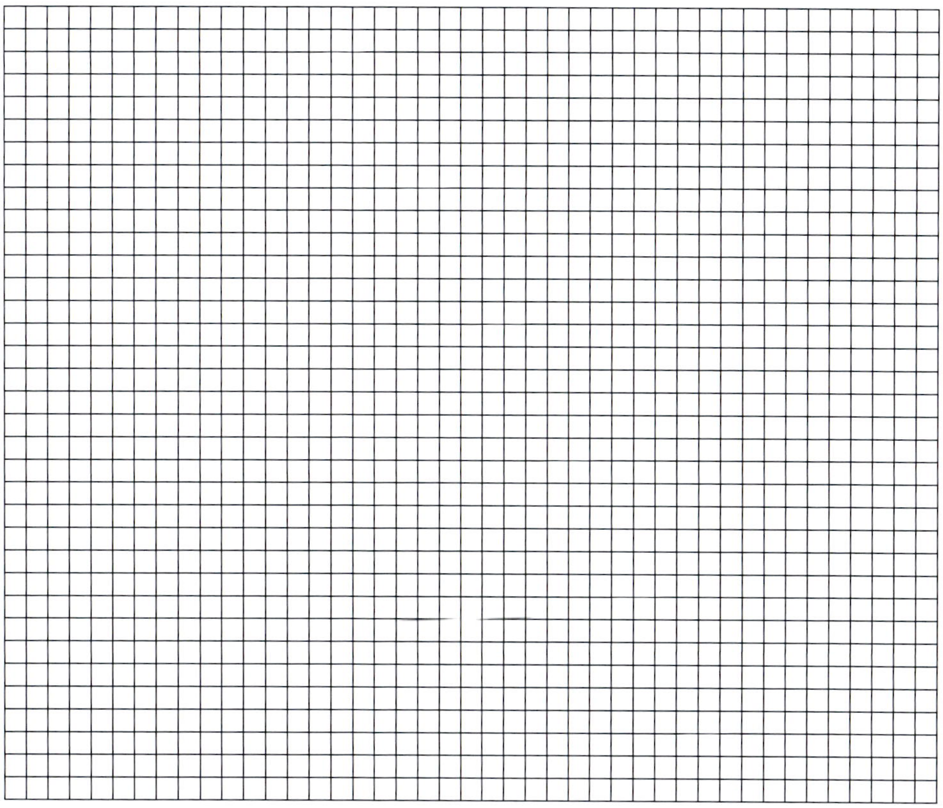

CHICKEN COASTER SET

COLOR KEY

- black - 1 yd
- red - 5 yds
- tan - 9 yds
- blue - 16 yds
- white - 10 yds
- dk blue - 10 yds
- yellow - 1 yd

DMC	COLOR
*blanc	white Fr. Knot - 5 yds

* Use 6 strands of floss.

Beak (12 x 8 threads)

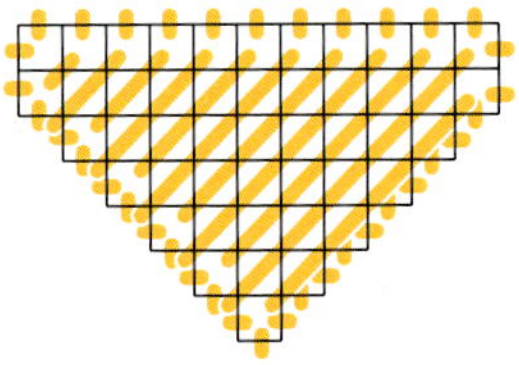

Caddy Front (28 x 27 threads)

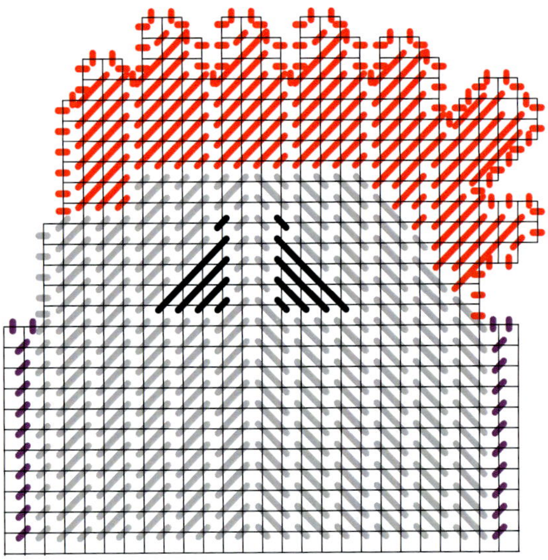

Caddy Back (27 x 12 threads)

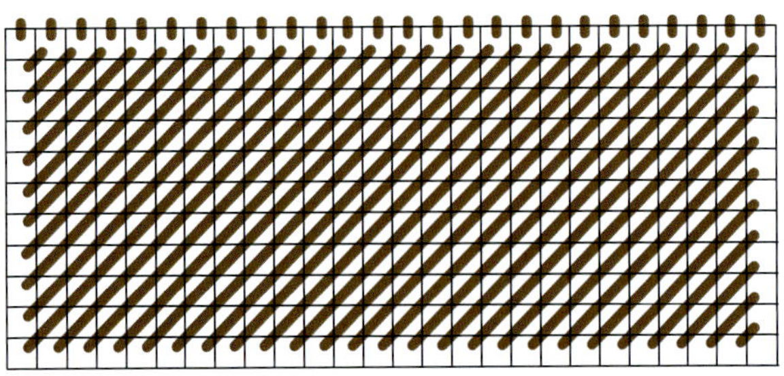

CHICKEN COASTER SET (shown on page 20)

Coaster Size: 3 3/4"w x 3 3/4"h

Caddy Size: 4"w x 4"h x 1 1/4"d

Supplies for Entire Set: Worsted weight yarn (refer to color key), DMC Embroidery Floss (refer to color key), one 10½" x 13½" sheet of 7 mesh plastic canvas, #16 tapestry needle, felt or cork (optional), and clear-drying craft glue (optional) and clear-drying craft glue (optional)

Stitches Used: French Knots, Gobelin Stitch, Overcast Stitch, Tent Stitch

Instructions:

1. Follow charts and use required stitches to work Chicken Coaster Set pieces.

2. Refer to photo for placement and tack Beak to Front using yellow yarn. To assemble Caddy pieces, join Front to Sides using tan yarn. Join Back to Sides using tan yarn. Join Bottom to Front using white yarn. Join Bottom to Back and Sides using tan yarn.

3. If backing is desired for Coasters, cut cork or felt slightly smaller than Coasters and glue to wrong side of stitched pieces.

Caddy Side (9 x 12 threads) (Stitch 2)

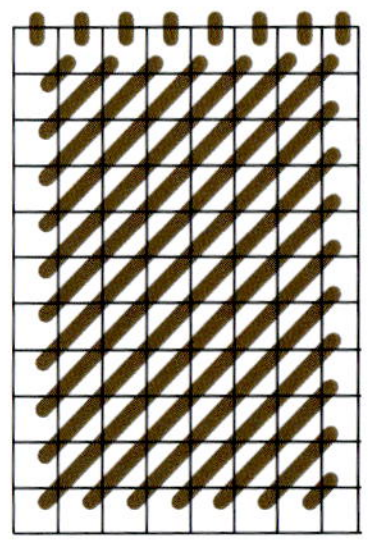

Caddy Bottom (27 x 9 threads)

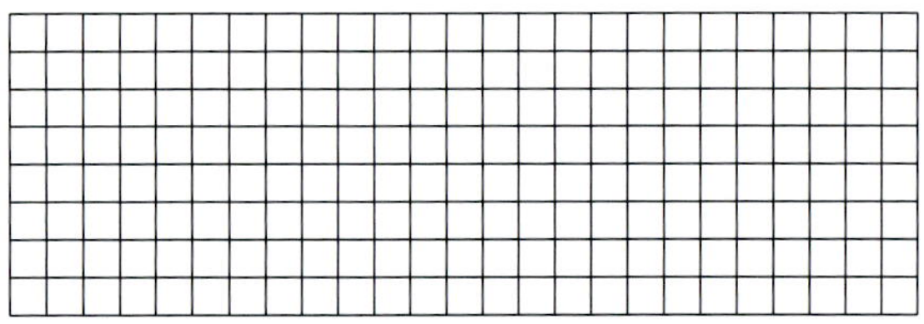

Coaster (26 x 26 threads) (Stitch 4)

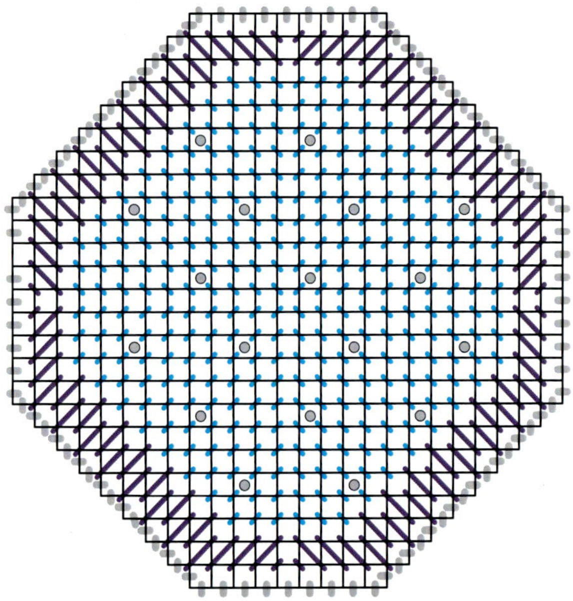

"EGGSIT" SIGN

"Eggsit" Sign (shown on page 20

Size: 3¼"w x 9½"h x ¾"d

Supplies: Worsted weight yarn (refer to color key), DMC Embroidery Floss (refer to color key), one 10½" x 13½" sheet of 7 mesh plastic canvas, #16 tapestry needle

Stitches Used: Backstitch, French Knots, Gobelin Stitch, Overcast Stitch, and Tent Stitch

Instructions:

1. Follow charts and use required stitches to work "Eggsit" Sign pieces. Before working Backstitch and French Knots, complete background with blue Tent Stitches as indicated on chart.

2. Matching ♥'s and ■'s, join Wing A and Wing B to Chicken using white yarn.

3. Refer to photo for placement to tack Chicken to "Eggsit" Sign using white yarn. Tack Heart to "Eggsit" Sign using red yarn.

COLOR KEY

- black - 1 yd
- red - 2 yds
- blue - 12 yds
- *white - 6 yds
- dk blue - 4 yds
- yellow - 1 yd
- *white Fr. Knot

* Use 2 plies of yarn for Backstitch and French Knot.

DMC	COLOR
*blanc	white Fr. Knot - 5 yds

* Use 6 strands of floss.

"Eggsit" Sign
(21 x 64 threads)

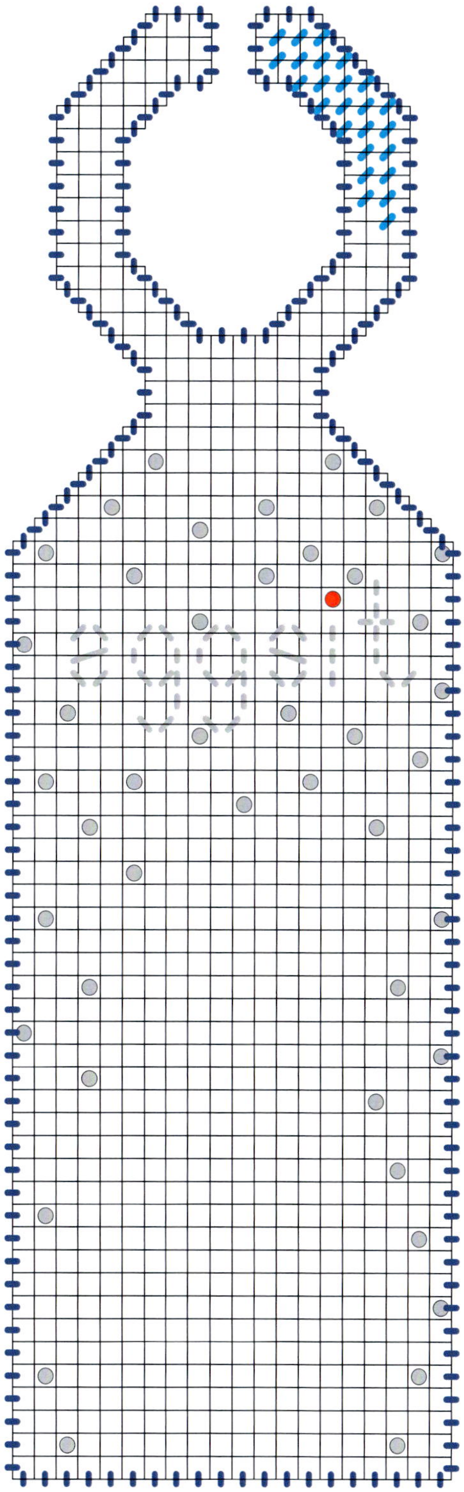

Chicken
(16 x 28 threads)

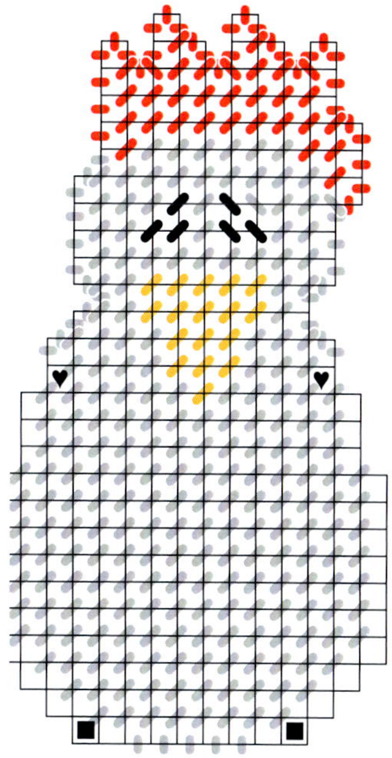

Wing A
(8 x 15 threads)

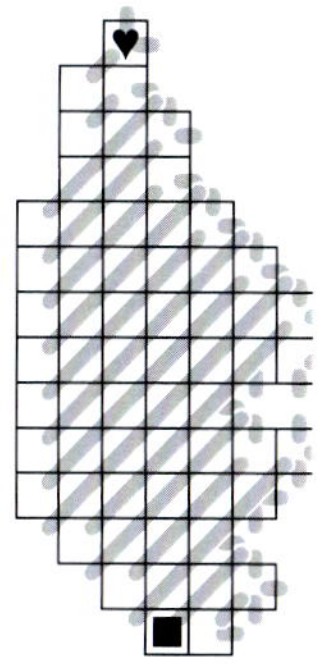

Wing B
(8 x 15 threads)

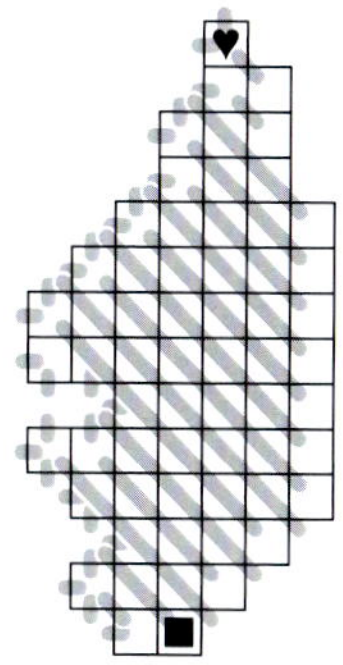

Heart
(8 x 7 threads)

Chicken "Coopon" Box

COLOR KEY

- black - 1 yd
- red - 3 yds
- blue - 28 yds
- *white - 8 yds
- dk blue - 4 yds
- yellow - 1 yd

* Use 2 plies of yarn for Backstitch.

DMC	COLOR
*blanc	white Fr. Knot - 2 yds

* Use 6 strands of floss.

CHICKEN "COOPON" BOX

Size: 6¾"w x 2"h x 4½"d

Supplies: Worsted weight yarn (refer to color key), DMC Embroidery Floss (refer to color key), two 10½" x 13½" sheets of 7 mesh plastic canvas, and #16 tapestry needle

Stitches Used: Backstitch, French Knot, Gobelin Stitch, Overcast Stitch, and Tent Stitch

Instructions:

1. Follow charts and use required stitches to work Chicken "Coopon" Box pieces. Before working Backstitches and French Knots, complete background of Top with blue Tent Stitches as indicated on chart.

2. Join Top Side A pieces to Top Side B pieces along short edges using blue yarn. Join Top to Top Sides using dk blue yarn.

3. Join Bottom Side A pieces to Bottom Side B pieces along short edges using blue yarn. Join Bottom to Bottom Sides using blue yarn.

4. Matching ♥'s and ■'s, join Wing A and Wing B to Chicken using white yarn.

5. Refer to photo for placement to tack Chicken to "Coopon" Box using white yarn. Tack Heart to "Coopon" Box using red yarn.

Heart
(8 x 7 threads)

Bottom Side B (43 x 10 threads) (Stitch 2)

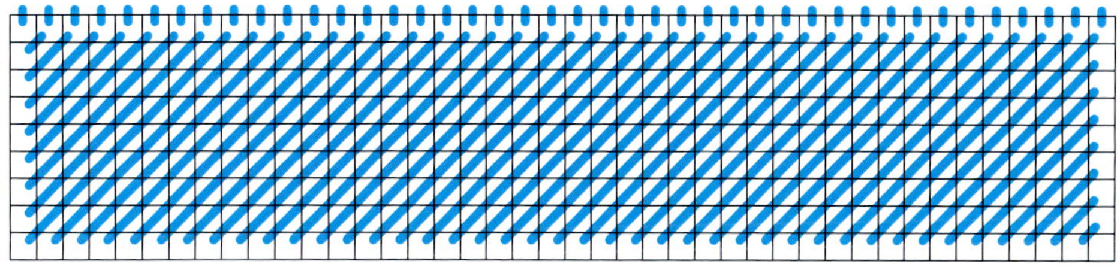

Bottom Side A (22 x 10 threads) (Stitch 2)

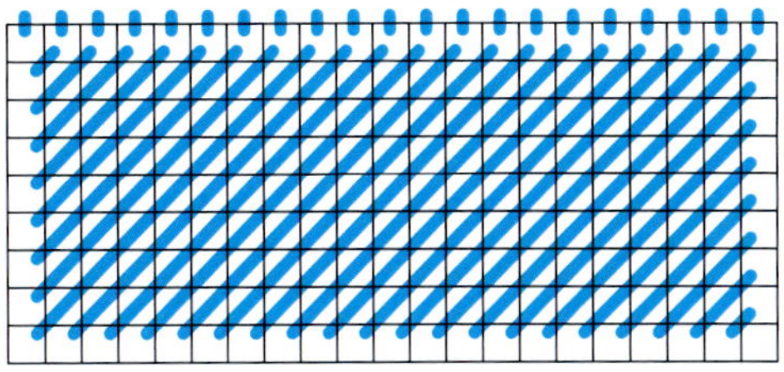

Bottom (43 x 22 threads)

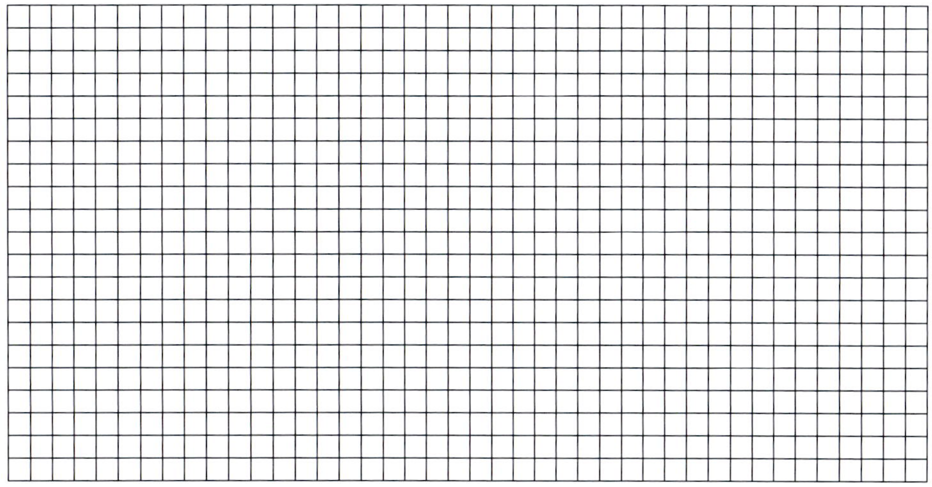

Wing A
(8 x 15 threads)

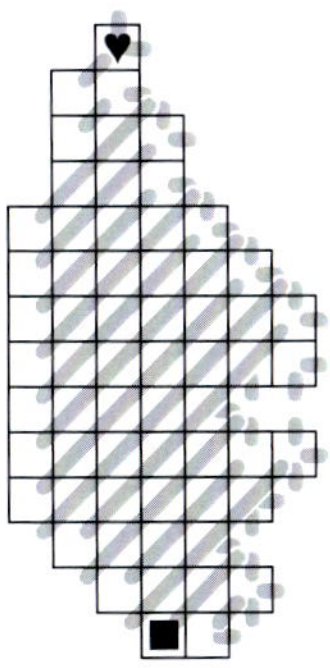

Wing B
(8 x 15 threads)

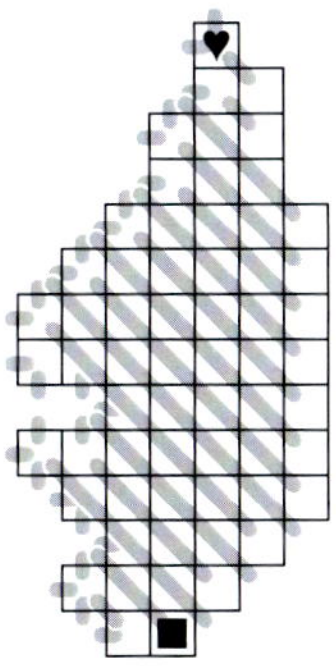

Top Side A (24 x 4 threads) (Stitch 2)

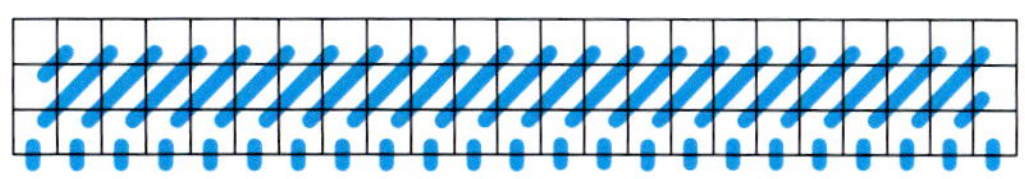

Top Side B (45 x 4 threads) (Stitch 2)

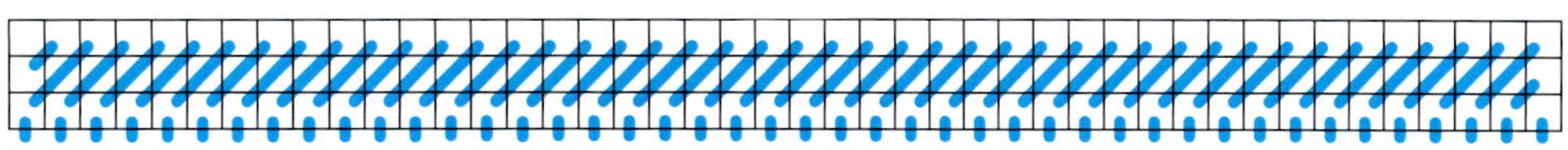

Chicken
(16 x 28 threads)

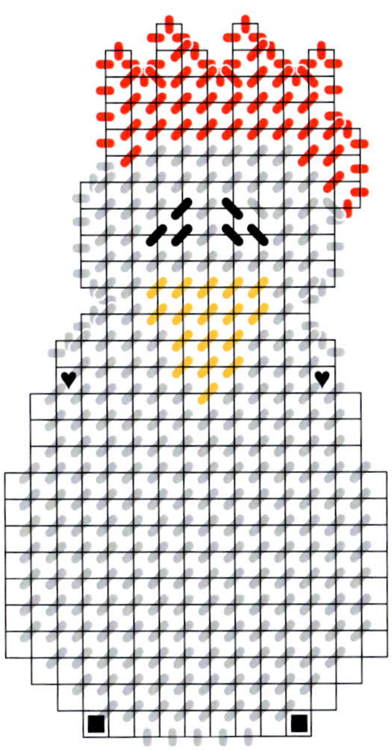

Top (45 x 24 threads)

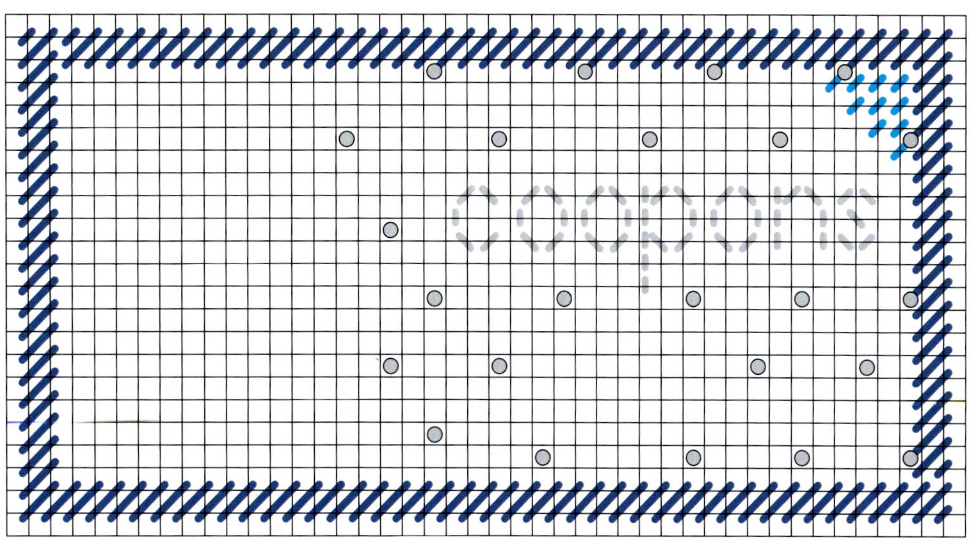

STAR & CHICKEN

COLOR KEY
black - 1 yd
red - 1 yd
white - 5 yds
yellow - 2 yds

STAR AND CHICKEN PLANT POKES

Approx Height: 7"h

Chicken Size: 2"w x 2¾"h

Approx Star Size: 1½"w x 1½"h

Supplies: Worsted weight yarn (refer to color key), one 10½" x 13½" sheet of 7 mesh plastic canvas, #16 tapestry needle, seven wooden skewers, and clear-drying craft glue

Stitches Used: Gobelin Stitch, Overcast Stitch, Tent Stitch

Instructions:

1. Follow charts and use required stitches to work one set of Chicken pieces and six Star pieces.

2. For Chicken Plant Poke only, join Wing A and Wing B to Chicken matching ♥'s and ■'s and using white yarn.

3. Glue one wooden skewer to wrong side of each completed stitched piece.

4. Refer to photo for placement and insert plant pokes into can.

CHICKEN MAGNET

Chicken Size: 2"w x 2¾"h

Supplies: Worsted weight yarn (refer to color key), one 10½" x 13½" sheet of 7 mesh plastic canvas, #16 tapestry needle, magnetic strip, and clear-drying craft glue

Stitches Used: Gobelin Stitch, Overcast Stitch, Tent Stitch

Instructions:

1. Follow charts and use required stitches to work Chicken pieces.

2. Matching ♥'s and ■'s, join Wing A and Wing B to Chicken using white yarn.

3. Glue magnetic strip to wrong side of each completed stitched piece.

Chicken
(13 x 19 threads)

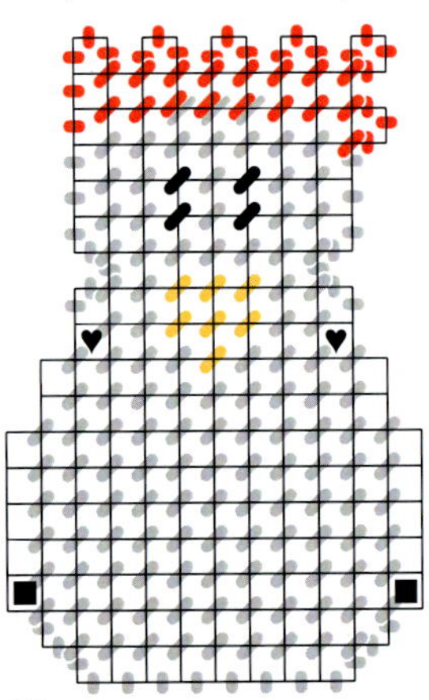

Wing A
(6 x 9 threads)

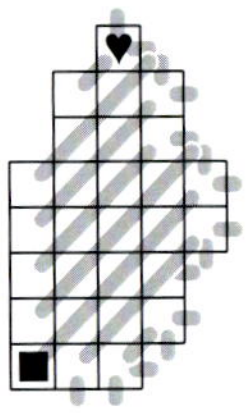

Wing B
(6 x 9 threads)

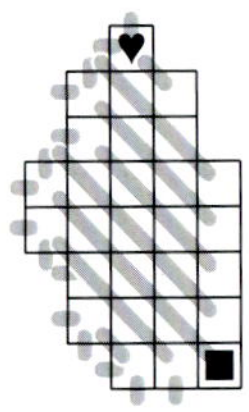

Star
(10 x 10 threads)

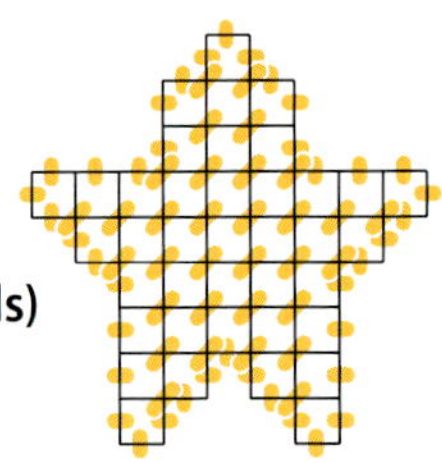

CHICKEN TOWEL HANGER

COLOR KEY
black - 1 yd
red - 5 yds
white - 6 yds
yellow - 1 yd

CHICKEN TOWEL HANGER

Size: 3¾"w x 6"h x ¾"d

Supplies: Worsted weight yarn (refer to color key), one 10½" x 13½" sheet of 7 mesh plastic canvas, #16 tapestry needle, 3" dia gold craft ring, ¾"w Velcro® brand fastener, sewing needle, and thread

Stitches Used: Gobelin Stitch, Overcast Stitch, Tent Stitch

Instructions:

1. Follow charts and use required stitches to work Chicken Towel Hanger pieces. *(**Note:** Back is not worked.)*

2. Refer to photo for placement and tack Beak to Front using yellow yarn.

3. For Hanger, cut a piece of plastic canvas 6 x 36 threads. *(**Note:** Hanger is not worked.)* Stitch a 1½" piece of hook (hard) Velcro® fastener to one end of Hanger using sewing needle and thread. Stitch a 1½" piece of loop (soft) Velcro® fastener to opposite end of Hanger using sewing needle and thread. Tack center of Hanger to center of Back.

4. Insert ring between Front and Back.

5. Join Front to Back using yarn color to match closest stitching area.

Beak (12 x 8 threads)

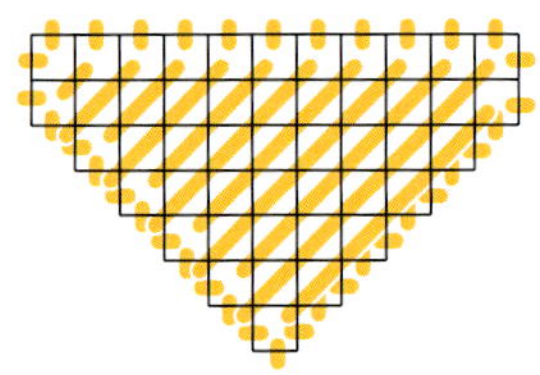

Front/Back (26 x 27 threads) (Cut 2, Stitch 1)

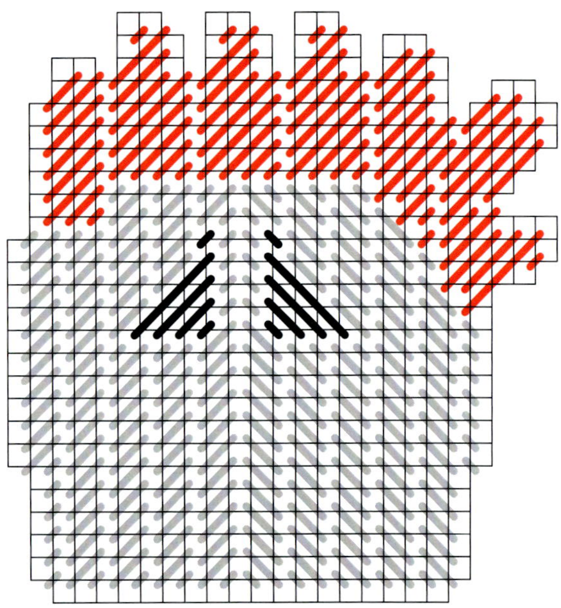

GENERAL INSTRUCTIONS

Working with Plastic Canvas

Counting Threads. The lines of the canvas are referred to as threads. Before cutting out the pieces, note the thread count of each chart listed above the chart, indicating the number of threads in the width and height. To cut plastic canvas pieces accurately, count **threads** (not **holes**) as shown in **Fig. 1**.

Fig. 1

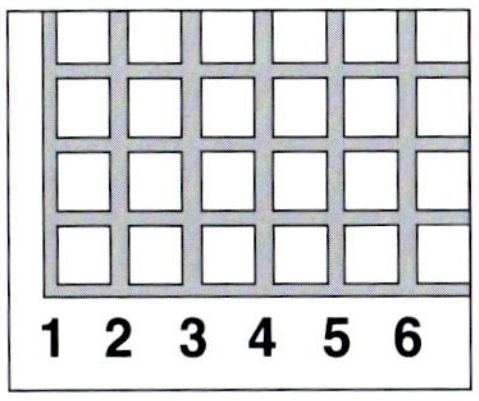

Marking the Canvas. You may use an overhead projector pen to mark the canvas. Outline shape with pen, cut out shape, and remove markings before stitching.

Cutting the Canvas. Cut as close to the thread as possible without cutting into the thread. If you don't cut close enough, "nubs" or "pickets" will be left on the edge. Make sure to cut all nubs from the canvas before stitching because nubs will snag the yarn and are difficult to cover. A craft knife is helpful when cutting a small area from the center of a larger piece of canvas. When using a craft knife, protect the table below with a layer of cardboard.

When cutting canvas along a diagonal, cut through the center of each intersection. This will leave enough plastic canvas on both sides of the cut so that both pieces may be used. Properly cut diagonal corners will be less likely to snag yarn and are easier to cover.

Working with Yarn & Embroidery Floss

Most brands of medium weight yarn have plies which are twisted together to form one strand. When the instructions indicate two plies of yarn, separate the strand of yarn and stitch using two of the plies.

DMC embroidery floss is made up of six strands which are twisted together. To ensure smoother stitches, separate strands and realign them before threading needle.

Reading the Color Key

A color key is included for each project, indicating the color used for each stitch on the chart. Additional information may also be given for when to use 2 ply yarn or embroidery floss.

Reading the Chart

When possible, the drawing on the chart looks like the completed stitch. For example, the tent stitches on the chart are drawn diagonally across an intersection of threads just as they look on the piece. When a stitch cannot be clearly drawn on the chart, like a French Knot, a symbol will be used instead.

Stitching the Design

Securing the First and Last Stitches. Don't knot the end of your yarn before you begin stitching. Instead, begin each length of yarn by coming up from the wrong side of the canvas and leaving a 1"-2" tail on the wrong side. Hold this tail against the canvas and work the first few stitches over the tail. When secure, clip the tail close to the stitched piece. Long tails can become tangled in future stitches or can show through to the right side of the canvas. After all the stitches of one color in an area are complete, end by running the needle under several stitches on the back. Trim the end close to the stitched piece.

Using Even Tension. Keep your stitching tension consistent, with each stitch lying flat and even. Pulling or yanking the yarn causes the tension to be too tight, and you will be able to see through your project. If the tension is too loose, the stitches won't lie flat. Most stitches tend to twist yarn. Drop your needle and let the yarn untwist occasionally.

Joining Pieces

Straight Edges. To join two or more pieces along a straight edge, place one piece on top of the other with right or wrong sides together. Make sure the edges are even, then overcast the pieces together through all layers.

Tacking. To tack pieces, run your needle under the backs of some stitches on one stitched piece to secure the yarn. Then run the needle through the canvas or under stitches on the piece to be tacked in place. This should securely attach pieces without tacking stitches showing.

Uneven Edges. When you join a diagonal edge to a straight edge, the holes will not line up exactly. Keep the pieces even and stitch through the holes as many times as necessary to completely cover the canvas.

Stitch Diagrams

*Unless otherwise indicated, bring needle up at **1** and all **odd** numbers and down at **2** and all **even** numbers.*

Backstitch

This stitch is worked over completed stitches to outline or define (**Fig. 2**). It is sometimes worked over more than one thread. It can also be used to cover canvas (**Fig. 3**).

Fig. 2

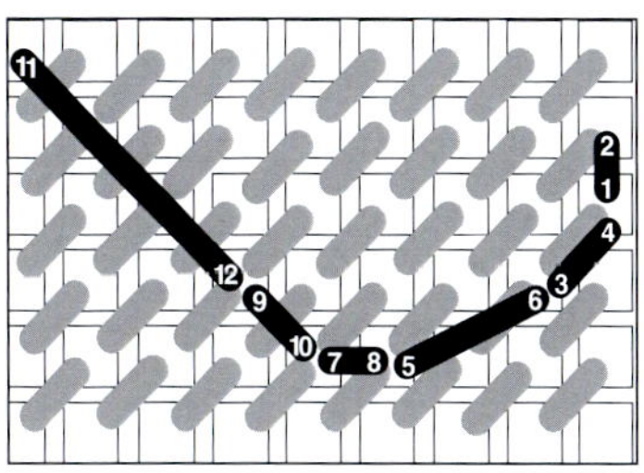

Fig. 3

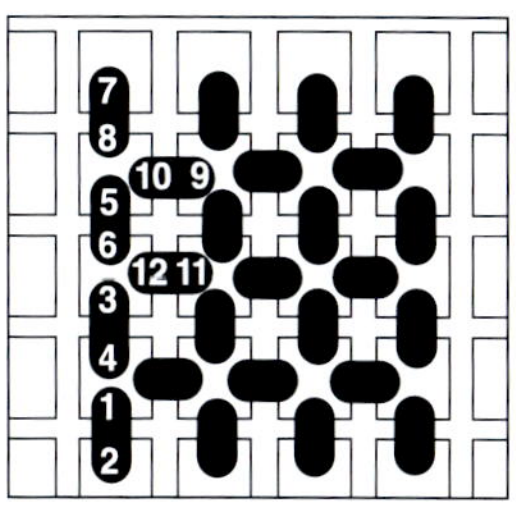

French Knot

Bring needle up through hole. Wrap yarn once around needle and insert needle in same hole, holding end of yarn with non-stitching fingers (**Fig. 4**). Tighten knot; then pull needle through canvas, holding yarn until it must be released.

Fig. 4

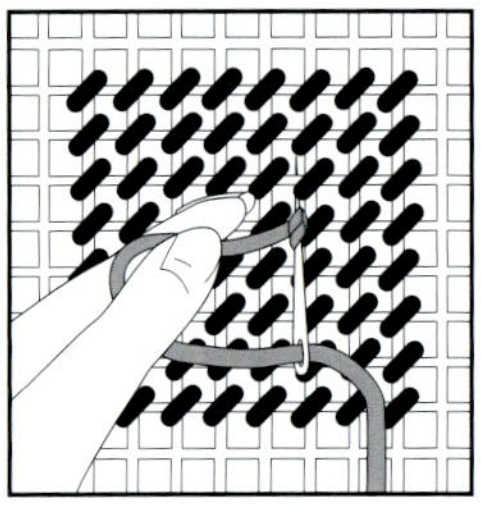

Gobelin Stitch

This straight stitch is worked over two or more threads or intersections (**Fig. 5**). The number of threads or intersections may vary according to the chart.

Fig. 5

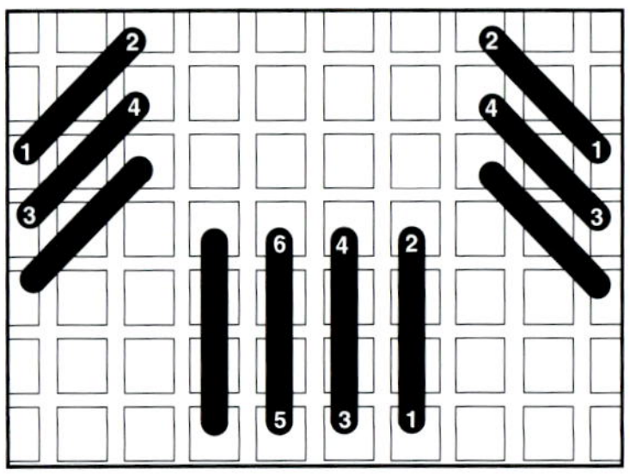

Overcast Stitch

This stitch covers the edge of canvas and joins pieces (**Fig. 6**). It may be necessary to go through the same hole more than once to get even coverage on the edge, especially at the corners.

Fig. 6

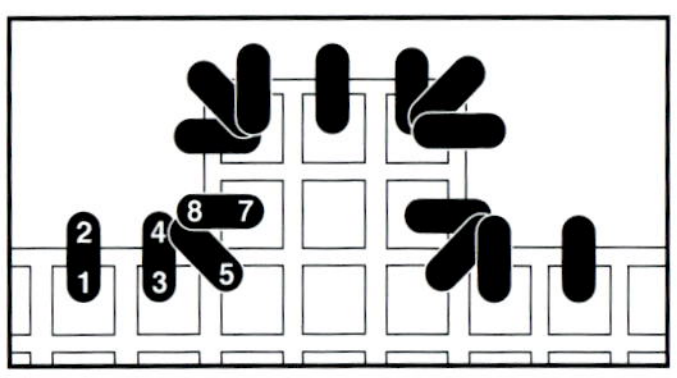

Scotch Stitch

This series of slanted stitches forms squares (**Fig. 7**).

Fig. 7

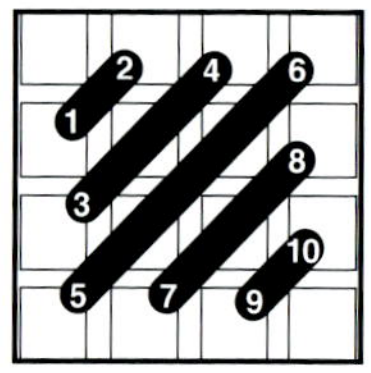

Tent Stitch

This stitch is worked in horizontal or vertical rows over one intersection (**Fig. 8**). Refer to **Fig. 9** to work the reversed tent stitch.

Fig. 8

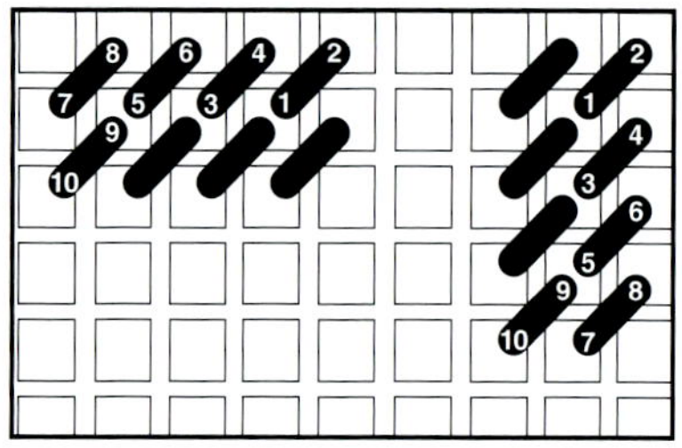

Fig. 9

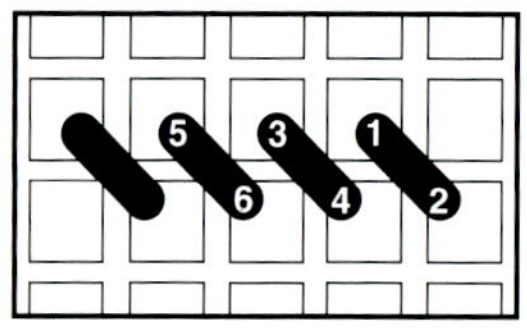

Made in U.S.A.